Grammar
Step by Step

3

Helen Kalkstein Fragiadakis

Ellen Rosenfield

Suzan Tiemroth-Zavala

with Chants by Carolyn Graham

Dedicated to our families, with enormous gratitude
for their patience and support, and to our students, with
great appreciation for their inspiration over the years.

Grammar Step by Step 3, 1st Edition

Published by McGraw-Hill ESL/ELT, a business unit of The McGraw-Hill
Companies, Inc., 1221 Avenue of the Americas, New York, NY 10020. Copyright
© 2005 by the McGraw-Hill Companies, Inc. All rights reserved. No part of this
publication may be reproduced or distributed in any form or by any means, or
stored in a database or retrieval system, without the prior written consent of The
McGraw-Hill Companies, Inc., including, but not limited to, in any network or
other electronic storage or transmission, or broadcast for distance learning.

ISBN: 0-07-284526-0
1 2 3 4 5 6 7 8 9 QPD/QPD 11 10 09 08 07 06 05

ISBN: 0-07-111071-2 (International Student Edition)
1 2 3 4 5 6 7 8 9 QPD/QPD 11 10 09 08 07 06 05

Editorial director: Tina B. Carver
Executive editor: Erik Gundersen
Senior developmental editor: Mari Vargo
Developmental editor: Jennifer Wilson Cooper
Production manager: Juanita Thompson
Cover designer: Delgado and Company, Inc.
Interior designer: Wee Design Group
Art: Tim Jones, Seitu Hayden, and Rich Stergulz
Skills indexer: Susannah MacKay

INTERNATIONAL EDITION ISBN 0-07-111071-2
Copyright © 2005. Exclusive rights by The McGraw Hill Companies, Inc., for
manufacture and export. This book cannot be re-exported from the country to
which it is sold by McGraw-Hill. The International Edition is not available in
North America.

www.esl-elt.mcgraw-hill.com

The **McGraw·Hill** Companies

Acknowledgements

The authors and publisher would like to thank the following individuals who reviewed the Grammar Step by Step program at various stages of development and whose comments, reviews, and assistance were instrumental in helping us shape the project:

Tony Albert
Jewish Vocational Services
San Francisco, CA

Gail Barta
West Valley College
Saratoga, CA

Joan Bornheimer
New Brunswick Board of
Education
New Brunswick, NJ

Gerald Lee Boyd
Northern Virginia Community
College
Annandale, VA

Christine Bunn
City College of San Francisco
San Francisco, CA

Inocencia Dacumos
West Contra Costa Adult
Education & Contra Costa College
Richmond/San Pablo, CA

Renee Eliscu
Tenafly Public Schools
Tenafly, NJ

Judith Garcia
Miami-Dade Community College
Miami, FL

Greg Keech
City College of San Francisco
San Francisco, CA

Susannah O. Mackay
Atlanta, GA

Veronica McGowen
University of Central Florida
Orlando, FL

Elizabeth Minicz
William Rainey Harper College
Glendale Heights, IL

Denise Phillips
Hudson County Community College
Jersey City, NJ

Meredith Pike-Baky
Education Task Force
San Rafael, CA

Jeanette Roy
Miami-Dade County Public
Schools
Miami, FL

Christina Schafermeyer
San Francisco, CA

Stephen Sloan
James Monroe High School
North Hills, CA

Colleen Weldele
Palomar College
San Marcos, CA

A note from the authors:

We worked with a fantastic team and would like to express our gratitude to everyone. Thank you to Tina Carver and McGraw-Hill for supporting this project. To Erik Gundersen, Executive Editor, and Mari Vargo, Senior Developmental Editor, thank you for your consistent support and exceptionally high professional standards. To Jennifer Wilson Cooper, our Developmental Editor, the words *thank you* cannot adequately express our appreciation for your daily support, guidance, and creativity. Your deep knowledge of the subject matter and our target audience has helped us to create the very best we can do, and we thank you for that. A big thank you also goes to our students who, with their insightful questions over the years, have inspired us to look more closely at our native language and to teach it as clearly and as engagingly as possible.

Table of Contents

LESSON		CONTEXT	PAGE

To the Teacher

Dear Colleagues,

As you know, our students are faced with all sorts of language input, and they depend on us to help them sort out the information that comes their way at school, at work, and in their daily lives. In the *Grammar Step by Step series*, we have divided grammatical information into digestible chunks that students can understand, and we have then provided practice in exercises that also develop listening, speaking, reading, vocabulary, and writing skills.

With Book 3, we have zeroed in on ways to teach grammar clearly and systematically and to isolate common areas of confusion in the high-intermediate grammar class. For example, we help students distinguish between *do* as an auxiliary and *do* as a main verb. We help students recognize and understand the use of the base form of the verb by having them analyze how it is used with questions, negative statements, modals and infinitives.

We have worked to create material that not only goes step by step but also engages students with familiar and sometimes humorous contexts. Our contexts are varied, and the characters we portray reflect a wide range of backgrounds and ages. While the vocabulary we use is controlled so as not to distract from the grammar being studied, we have made an effort to use common and natural language that is essential for communication.

As our students work to learn English, we strive to keep them motivated, involved, and rewarded, and to provide them with material that helps make sense of the chaos of language. We sincerely hope that, with *Grammar Step by Step*, your students will find some order in the chaos and have fun at the same time.

Helen Kalkstein Fragiadakis   Carolyn Graham

Ellen Rosenfield   Suzan Tiemroth-Zavala

Overview of *Grammar Step by Step*

Grammar Step by Step 3 is the third in a three-level series of beginning to high-intermediate books offering extensive grammar practice for young adult and adult learners. In *Grammar Step by Step*, small chunks of grammar are presented and practiced on a series of two-page spreads. While grammar presentation charts in many books present students with more new grammar than they can handle, the charts in *Grammar Step by Step* are designed to streamline the presentation of new grammar.

Each lesson in *Grammar Step by Step* features thorough practice of a grammar point, leading from controlled to open-ended activities. There are abundant opportunities for students to personalize learning through engaging speaking and writing tasks. Both lesser-trained and more experienced teachers will find the fresh and varied activity types meaningful and effective while enjoying the comfort of the accessible and predictable format.

Grammar Step by Step presents the content that experienced teachers expect to find in a grammar series with a number of distinguishing features.

- **Flexible two-page lesson structure** allows teachers to select from a comprehensive array of lessons according to student and curricular needs.

- **Integrated skills approach to grammar** features initial listening activities that establish the grammar focus for reading, writing, and speaking tasks.

- **Carolyn Graham's chants** focus student attention on the oral/aural dimension of grammar learning while making classes lively and motivating.

- **Classroom-tested grammar points** target classic trouble spots, such as accurately using *have / do / make / take*.

- **Engaging illustrations** in each lesson visually define key vocabulary, allowing teachers and students to focus on grammar learning.

- **Resource-rich Teacher's Manual** reduces teacher prep time with reproducible tests and 64 expansion activities—one for each two-page lesson.

Components

The complete *Grammar Step by Step 3* program includes the following components:

- Student Book
- Teacher's Manual with answer key, 64 reproducible expansion activities, and a review test for each group of lessons
- Audiocassette/audio CD with recordings of all listening scripts and all chants, featuring Carolyn Graham

Guide to *Grammar Step by Step*

Each streamlined two-page lesson follows a **predictable and accessible format**.

The opening activity of each lesson acquaints students with the grammar point through a **context-building listening activity**.

Engaging art illustrates contexts and teaches **new vocabulary words**.

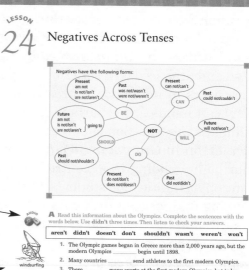

LESSON

24 Negatives Across Tenses

Negatives have the following forms:

Present
am not
is not/isn't
are not/aren't

Past
was not/wasn't
were not/weren't

Present
can not/can't

Past
could not/couldn't

CAN

Future
am not
is not/isn't
are not/aren't
going to

BE

Future
will not/won't

NOT

WILL

SHOULD

DO

Past
should not/shouldn't

Present
do not/don't
does not/doesn't

Past
did not/didn't

🔊 AUDIO

A Read this information about the Olympics. Complete the sentences with the words below. Use **didn't** three times. Then listen to check your answers.

| aren't | didn't | doesn't | don't | shouldn't | wasn't | weren't | won't |

windsurfing

1. The Olympic games began in Greece more than 2,000 years ago, but the modern Olympics _____ begin until 1898.

2. Many countries _____ send athletes to the first modern Olympics.

3. There _____ many sports at the first modern Olympics, but today, there are hundreds of sports.

4. Not every sport is played in the Olympics. For example, windsurfing is an Olympic sport, but skateboarding and golf _____

skateboarding

5. A long time ago, women _____ participate in the Olympics.

6. Some countries still _____ send women athletes to the Olympics.

7. Now soccer is popular in the U.S., but it _____ popular 30 years ago.

8. The U.S. has many good Olympic teams, but it _____ always have the best teams.

medal winner

9. The 2012 Olympics _____ be in New York. They might be in Paris.

10. Some people think that Olympic medal winners _____ be able to make a lot of money in advertisements.

72

B Karina doesn't know a lot about sports. She is talking to Jean. Complete their conversation with the correct negative form of the verb in parentheses.

Karina: I think baseball will be the number one sport in France.

Jean: I disagree. Baseball (1. be) _won't be_ the number one sport. Soccer will be the most popular sport there for years to come.

Karina: I think American football and soccer are the same.

Jean: No, American football and soccer (2. be) _____ the same. In fact, they're completely different.

Karina: Can soccer players throw the ball?

Jean: Well, the goalie can throw the ball, but the other soccer players (3. touch) _____ the ball with their hands.

Karina: That's interesting. I think Pele is a soccer player from Argentina. Am I right?

Jean: Well, Pele is a soccer player, but he (4. be) _____ from Argentina. He's from Brazil.

Karina: I think the United States won the World Cup last year.

Jean: No. The United States (5. win) _____ the World Cup last year. You know, you (6. know) _____ much about sports, Karina!

Karina: But I'm trying to learn. You (7. laugh) _____ at me!

C Change these statements to **yes-no** questions. Walk around and ask classmates the questions. When students say **No**, write their names on the lines. Then on a separate piece of paper, write seven negative sentences about your classmates.

| **Yes-No Questions** | **Students Who Answer "No"** |

1. You were a good athlete when you were a child.
Were you a good athlete when you were a child? _____

2. You played baseball or soccer when you were a child. _____

3. You could swim fast when you were a child. _____

4. You love sports. _____

5. You are a good athlete. _____

6. You are taking an exercise class now. _____

7. You think you should watch sports on TV every Saturday. _____

73

Tightly controlled exercises allow students to focus on the structure of the new grammar point.

Open-ended activities or chants at the close of each lesson provide opportunities to personalize the grammar point or interact with the grammar in an engaging way.

x

Clear and concise charts introduce grammar points in easily comprehensible chunks.

Audiocassettes and audio CDs contain at least one listening activity per lesson, as well as 30 original chants written and recorded by Carolyn Graham.

LESSON
20

Contrast: *Do* as Main Verb and *Do* as Helping Verb

Do, does, and **did** can be helping verbs or main verbs.

Do as a Helping Verb		*Do* as a Main Verb
Negatives	**Questions**	I always do my best.
I don't study.	Do you study?	She does the shopping.
He doesn't study. (When)	Does he study?	We did our laundry.
They didn't study.	Did they study?	I'm doing fine.

Do as a Helping Verb with *Do* as a Main Verb	
Negatives:	She doesn't do anything around the house.
	He didn't do a good job.
Questions:	Do you do your best at school?
	When did you do your chores?

Common phrases with do: do the laundry, do the shopping, do the dishes, do your work, do something, do nothing, not do anything, do a good job, do homework, do your best, do someone a favor, do chores

A John is talking on the phone with his mother about his roommate. Complete their conversation by filling in each line with a form of **do**. Then listen to check your answers.

Mom: How are you doing?
John: I'm (1.) _____doing_____ fine.
Mom: How's your roommate Paul?
John: He's OK, but he's not a very neat person. He (2.) (not) _____ anything around the house.
Mom: What do you mean?
John: Well, he likes to cook, but after he eats, he never (3.) _____ the dishes. And he never (4.) _____ his laundry. His dirty clothes are in a big pile next to his bed.
Mom: Oh, my! (5.) _____ you tell him to clean up?
John: Yes, I asked him to wash the dishes last night, but he (6.) (not) _____ them. He just left the dishes in the sink.
Mom: That's terrible. (7.) _____ you wash your dishes, John?
John: Of course, Mom. I always clean up!
Mom: Well, tell Paul that he has to do something around the house. Tell him if he (8.) (not) _____ any chores, you'll look for a new roommate. By the way, how's school? (9.) _____ you have a lot of homework?
John: Yes. In fact, I'm (10.) _____ my homework right now.

60

B Write the answers from Exercise A on the lines. Check **HV** if the answer is a helping verb, **MV** if it is a main verb, or both if the answer includes both.

		HV	MV			HV	MV
1.	doing		✓	6.			
2.	doesn't do	✓	✓	7.			
3.				8.			
4.				9.			
5.				10.			

C Write sentences about John and his roommate to complete the chart.

	Affirmative	Negative	Yes-No Question
Singular/ Present	John does his homework every day.	John _____	_____ ?
Plural/ Present	They _____	They don't do their homework every day.	_____ ?
Singular/ Past	He _____	He _____	Did he do his homework yesterday?
Plural/ Past	They did their homework yesterday.	They _____	_____ ?

Reminder Notes provide students with information that will help them complete the exercises.

Remember the possessive adjectives: "his" and "their."

D Chant

The Poet

Do you know the poet Thomas Jones?
Of course I do.
I love his poems.
I do too.
Does he publish a lot?
No, he doesn't.
He didn't publish a thing last year.
Poets don't make money.
But how does he live?
How does he pay the rent?
He teaches.
What does he teach?
Poetry.

61

One lesson in each group ends with a **chant** which allows students to practice the **pronunciation, rhythm, and intonation** of the new grammar point.

Each group of lessons is followed by a **two-page *Review*** in which students can test their recollection and understanding of the preceding grammar points.

Most Reviews begin with a **dictation** which incorporates both new grammar and new vocabulary from the previous lessons.

Lessons 59–61

Review
Present Perfect Tense with *For, Since,* and *Ever*

A Dictation Karen is talking about love. Listen and write what you hear. Then underline the sentences in the present perfect tense. Circle the past participles. Put a box around **since** and **for**. Key words: *at first sight, immediately, guy, teenager*

Have you ever _____

B Look at the sentences below. Write **A** in the space on the left if the sentences go with diagram A; write **B** if they go with diagram B.

A We don't know when something happened in the past.

B Something started in the past and continues to the present.

___A_ 1. She has been divorced three times.
_____ 2. She has known the guy for only two weeks.
_____ 3. She has been this way since she was a teenager.
_____ 4. My brother has tried to give her advice many times.
_____ 5. I have told her to be careful more than once.

C On a separate piece of paper, rewrite part of the dictation from Exercise A. Write about twin cousins. Change **she** to **they, her** to **them**, and **guy** to **guys**.

FIRST SENTENCE: *My twin cousins always fall in love immediately, but . . .*

184

Review activities ask students to **synthesize the grammar** that they've learned.

D Robert is a lottery winner. Read about his good luck and how it has changed his life. Then write a question for each of the answers below.

Believe it or not, I have won the lottery twice! And since I won all that money, my life has changed a lot. I have been on TV five times. I have given my family lots of presents and they have thanked me. But I haven't spent all the money only on myself. I have helped my community, too.

1. *Has Robert ever won the lottery?*
Yes, Robert has won the lottery twice.

2. _____?
Yes, his life has changed a lot.

3. _____?
No, his family hasn't been on TV.

4. _____?
Yes, he has given his family many presents.

5. _____?
No, he hasn't spent money only on himself.

6. _____?
Yes, he has helped his community.

E What does the contraction in each sentence mean? Write **is** or **has** on each line to the left.

Has 1. She's fallen in love three times.
____ 2. She's in love again!
____ 3. He's given her a lot of advice.
____ 4. He's a good brother.
____ 5. It's an interesting story.
____ 6. It's been an interesting year.

F Find the mistakes. Make the corrections.

Has
1. ~~Have~~ he met many people?
2. Since I have come to the U.S., I've met a lot of people.
3. We have been in school since two years.
4. They have had free time rarely.
5. She has spoken English with her children never.
6. They've never be on an airplane.
7. I have learn a lot.
8. Has he gone to the city ever?

Error-correction activities allow students to identify and fix common errors that they might make themselves.

G On a separate piece of paper, rewrite these sentences. Change **since** to **for** and **for** to **since**. Imagine that it is 2 p.m. and that today's date is Tuesday, August 18th, 2020.

EXAMPLE: *I have been in the U.S. since 2018. I have been in the U.S. for two years.*

1. He hasn't seen his family for a long time.
2. She has been on vacation since August 4th.
3. I haven't spoken English since Sunday!
4. We have been in this room for four hours.
5. They have had a lot of work for a week.
6. I've known her since 2012.
7. You've been absent for 10 days.
8. Since Sunday, it has been very cold.

185

The **_Have Fun_ activities** following each group of lessons reward students for their hard work.

Puzzles, word games, and cooperative activities allow students to use the new grammar in fun and entertaining ways.

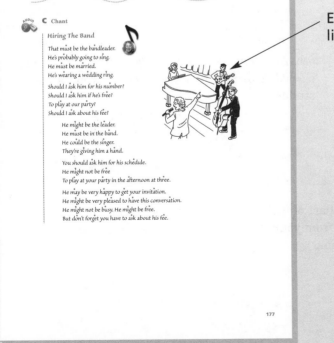

LESSONS
34–37

Have Fun

A Unscramble the letters to create comparative and superlative adjectives. Then use the numbered letters to find the secret message.

Irregular Comparative and Superlative Adjectives	1. EEBTRT	b e t t e r
	2. TSBE	8
	3. EATHRFR	f 7
	4. RAHTTFSE	t
	5. ESWRO	o
	6. RWOTS	8
	7. ESLE	10 8
	8. LASTE	l
Comparative Adjectives (-er)	9. DSADRE	d 8
	10. TOEHRT	o
	11. RIGEGB	g
	12. NIISERO	i 11
	13. IERAES	a
Superlative Adjectives (-est)	14. DLSTCEO	l 8
	15. SADETDS	d 3
	16. FTSUIENN	n 4
	17. HLTAESHIET	h
	18. TNESWE	w

My [ ] m[ ] [ ]
1 2 3 4 5
my [ ]
6 7 8 9 10 11

114

Each _Have Fun_ spread closes with a lively **chant by Carolyn Graham**.

C Chant

Hiring The Band

That must be the bandleader.
He's probably going to sing.
He must be married.
He's wearing a wedding ring.

Should I ask him for his number?
Should I ask him if he's free?
To play at our party?
Should I ask about his fee?

He might be the leader.
He must be in the band.
He could be the singer.
They're giving him a hand.

You should ask him for his schedule.
He might not be free
To play at your party in the afternoon at three.

He may be very happy to get your invitation.
He might be very pleased to have this conversation.
He might not be busy. He might be free.
But don't forget you have to ask about his fee.

177

The **resource-rich Teacher's Manual** reduces teacher prep time with reproducible tests and 64 expansion activities—one for each two-page lesson!

Getting to Know You
The First Class

A **Walk & Talk** Get to know your classmates. Write a **yes-no** question using the words in each box. Then walk around the classroom and ask your questions. When a student says, "Yes" or "Sometimes," write his or her name in the box. If a student says, "No," just say, "Thank you."

EXAMPLE:
A: *Is this your first time at this school?*   A: *Is this your first time at this school?*
B: *No, it's not.*   B: *Yes, it is.*
A: *OK. Thank you.*   A: *Great! What's your first name?*
                                   How do you spell it?

first time/your/ is/this/at this school	happy/you are/today	work/you/do	job/like/you/do/ your	grammar/like/ do/you
Is this your first time at this school?				
name	name	name	name	name
you/homework/ a lot/do/of/want	afraid/tests/you/ of/are	want/vacation/ do/a/you	TV shows/do/ understand/ you/in English	listen/ever/do/ to/you/radio/ the/in English
name	name	name	name	name
computer/you/a/ use/do/how/to/ know	email/have/an/ you/do/address	other/know/you/ class/do/this/in/ students	dictionary/good/ do/have/you/a	games/do/play/ you/to/like
name	name	name	name	name

With the other students, put this chart on the board with a collection of student names in each box. Get more information from your classmates by asking them to explain why they answered, "Yes" to the questions.

B Writing In a letter, introduce yourself to your classmates. You can write about any of the following topics: family, job, interests, plans, or hobbies.

(date) ....

Dear Classmates,

     I would like to tell you about myself. I ....

....

....

....

....

....

....

....

....

....

....

                               Here's to a good time together!

                               ....

C Conversation Work with a partner or small group. Take turns reading your letters to each other. Your classmates will listen to you and then ask questions to get more details about you.

After you finish your conversation, each student will tell the class one interesting thing about one other student.

I would like to introduce .... *. She / He* .... *.*

Introduction

Words to Know	Examples
1. a chart (with columns)		the left column	the middle column	the right column	
2. a phrase (= a group of words)	from now on, of course, as usual
3. a clause (= a group of words with a subject and a verb. The first example is a sentence. The second example is not.)	I like teaching. . . because it's rewarding. clause clause (sentence) (not a sentence)
4. a sentence (= a group of words with a subject and a verb)	My name is Suzanne. I like teaching and writing textbooks.
5. a paragraph (= a group of sentences related to the same idea)	My name is Suzanne. I'm from southern California, but now I live in northern California. I have been teaching English for a long time.
6. a timeline	←————————————————→ 1995 2000 2005 2010 2020
7. a team (= a group that competes with another group, like in sports)	Half the class will be on Team X, and the other half will be on Team O.

Directions	Example
1. Check the correct answer.	✓
2. Put ∅ when no word is needed.	__∅__ China is a beautiful country.
3. Unscramble the letters.	HLINEGS ---> English
4. Match the words on the left with the correct word on the right.	__b__ 1. ham and a. jelly __a__ 2. peanut butter and b. eggs
5. Use the word in parentheses.	(1. want) She _wants_ to learn English.
6. Take turns.	You ask three questions, and then I'll ask three questions.
7. Pretend.	Why don't you pretend to be a famous actor, and I'll be a reporter?
8. Imagine.	It is the year 2020. My English is excellent.

A Unscramble the words. For ideas, look at the words in the chart on page 4. Use the numbered letters to find the secret message.

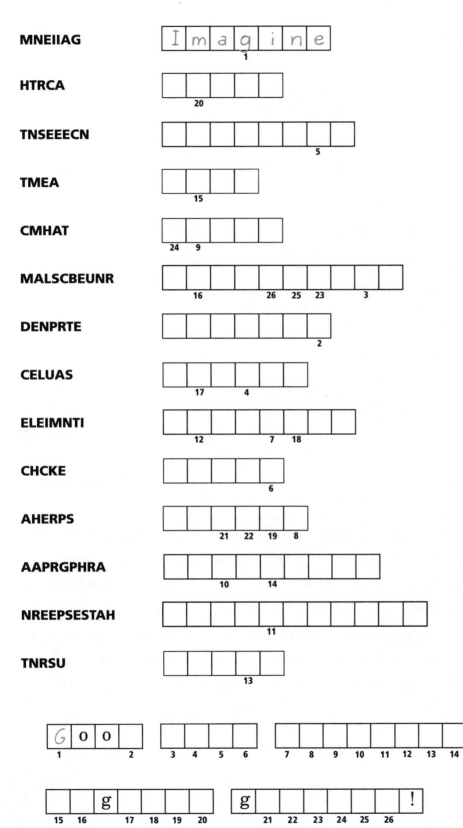

Nouns

Nouns are people, places, and things. *Things* include ideas and activities.

People		Places		Things	
Singular	**Plural**	**Singular**	**Plural**	**Singular**	**Plural**
a winner	the winners	a school	the schools	a prize	some prizes

Language Notes:
Proper nouns are names. They start with a capital letter. Proper nouns include the names of people, places, months, days, and holidays.
Carla, Academy High School, May, Monday, Labor Day.

Some word endings show that a word is a noun.
-tion/-sion   informa**tion**, ques**tion**, conversa**tion**, deci**sion**
-ment   appoint**ment**, announce**ment**, apart**ment**
-er*   teach**er**, winn**er**, fath**er**
*Some –**er** words are *not* nouns: oth**er**, old**er**, aft**er**.

These words often come before nouns:
Before singular nouns: *a/an/the; one; my/your/his/her/our/their*
Before plural nouns: *the; two/three; my/your/his/her/our/their; some/many*

A Read the principal's announcements. Look at the **bolded** words. Some are nouns and some are not. Circle the nouns. Then listen.

Welcome back to Academy High School. I **hope** you had a good **vacation**. I have a few **announcements**. First, pick up your **schedules** in the **office**. Second, don't **forget** that our **school** is closed next **Monday** for **Labor Day**. Third, I have some **very** exciting news. Last **week**, Carla Matos **won** a **prize** for her **wonderful composition**. She and **three** other **winners** are going on a **trip** to **Hawaii** for two **weeks** in **December**. The **teachers** are all very proud of **Carla**. We are **having** a **party** for her today **and** everyone is invited. OK now, before I end my announcements, are there any **questions**?

B Put each noun that you circled from Exercise A in the correct column.

Proper nouns	Singular nouns	Plural nouns
1. _Academy High School_	7. _vacation_	15. _announcements_
2. _____	8. _____	16. _____
3. _____	9. _____	17. _____
4. _____	10. _____	18. _____
5. _____	11. _____	19. _____
6. _____	12. _____	20. _____
	13. _____	
	14. _____	

C Add two nouns to each column below. Use singular and plural nouns. Show your list to a classmate. Add your classmate's nouns to your list.

Things you can see in the classroom	Holidays	Prizes you would like to win
desks	Labor Day	a boat
a window	Thanksgiving	money

Remember to capitalize proper nouns.

D Work in a group of three students. In three minutes, write as many nouns as you can think of that end with **-tion**, **-sion**, **-ment**, and **-er**. The group with the most words wins.

-tion/-sion	-ment	-er
nation	announcement	teacher
_____	_____	_____
_____	_____	_____
_____	_____	_____

LESSON

2 Adjectives

Adjectives are words that describe nouns.

- Adjectives come before nouns.

Correct	**Incorrect**
It's a beautiful view.	~~It's a view beautiful.~~

- Adjectives come after the verb **BE** (*am, is, are, was, were*) and the verbs **feel**, **look**, and **sound**.
- Adjectives come after the verb **get**, when **get** means **become**.

Correct	**Incorrect**
The hotel is comfortable.	~~The hotel comfortable.~~
I feel tired.	~~I tired.~~
The beach gets crowded.	~~The beach crowded.~~

- Adjectives have no plural form.

Correct	**Incorrect**
Vacations are expensive.	~~Vacations are expensives.~~

- Use **a** or **an** when the adjective comes before a singular noun.
  Don't use **a** or **an** when the adjective is alone.

Correct	**Incorrect**
She is a lucky woman.	~~She is lucky woman.~~
She is lucky.	~~She is a lucky.~~

- Some adjectives end in **-ed** or **-ing**. Don't confuse these adjectives with verbs or gerunds.
  I feel tired.   It's an exciting trip.

A Read Carla's postcard from Hawaii. Underline the adjectives. Then listen.

Dear Everyone,
   I'm having a <u>wonderful</u> time. The weather is perfect. It's hot and sunny in the afternoon, but at night it gets cool. I swim and rest all day. I feel so happy here!
   My hotel room is very comfortable and quiet, and I have a beautiful view of the beach. I love to sit on my balcony and watch the huge waves. And the food is delicious, especially the fresh pineapple. As you know, Hawaii is famous for pineapple.
   I love Hawaii! I was lucky to win this exciting trip.
   See you soon!
   Love, Carla

The Matos Family
244 Miles Dr.
Phoenix, AZ 85026

B Look at the underlined word in each of the sentences below. If the underlined word is an adjective, put a check mark (✓) on the line.

1. _____ Carla had a wonderful <u>vacation</u>.

2. _✓_ It was a very <u>exciting</u> trip.

3. _____ She went <u>swimming</u> every day.

4. _____ They <u>traveled</u> by plane.

5. _____ She wasn't <u>homesick</u>.

6. _____ They visited some <u>interesting</u> sights.

7. _____ The beach was <u>crowded</u>.

8. _____ She wasn't <u>disappointed</u> in her trip.

C Find the mistakes. Rewrite the sentences.

1. Hawaii very beautiful.   Hawaii is very beautiful.

2. The food delicious.   ....

3. Carla has a room very comfortable. ....

4. She is having wonderful vacation.   ....

5. Her boyfriend is a handsome.   ....

6. In Hawaii the waves are very bigs. ....

7. Hawaii famous for coffee.   ....

8. There are many stores expensive.   ....

9. It is wonderful place.   ....

D **Part 1** Read the paragraph about a famous place. Underline each adjective. Guess the name of this place.

   My favorite place is famous for tall buildings. The streets are very noisy and crowded. Some of the restaurants are very expensive. The weather is cold in the winter and hot in the summer. Many famous people live in this place.

This place is ....

Part 2 On a separate piece of paper, write a paragraph about your favorite place. Use the paragraph above as a model. Include at least one adjective in each sentence. Ask a partner to guess the name of your favorite place.

Verbs

Some verbs are words that can show actions in the present, past, and future. These are called *action verbs.*

I usually **drive** to work.   He **walked** to school yesterday.   We **won't arrive** late.

Some verbs do not show actions. These are called *non-action* verbs.

You **look** familiar.   The class **costs** a lot of money.

Verbs are often two words: a helping verb and a main verb.

	Helping Verb	**Main Verb**
I**'m waiting** for the bus.	'm	waiting
I **don't own** a car.	don't	own
Did the teacher **give** a lot of tests?	did	give
Will we **get** there?	will	get

BE verbs can also be main verbs.

He **is** busy.   The bus **was** here.   Will we **be** late?

Do can also be a main verb.

She **does** crossword puzzles at the bus stop.

Verbs have affirmative, negative, and question forms.

Jose **drives**.   Jose **doesn't drive**.   **Does** Jose **drive**?

A Read Mika and John's conversation. Underline the main verbs. Then listen. Practice the conversation with a partner.

Mika: Excuse me, does the M bus <u>stop</u> here?

John: Yes. I'm waiting for the same bus. It sometimes comes a little late.

Mika: I don't know the bus schedule because I usually drive.

John: Well, I hope the bus comes soon. My class starts in 15 minutes! Professor Fields hates it when we're late.

Mika: Are you in Mr. Field's English class?

John: Yes, I am. He's a great teacher. I like him very much.

Mika: He was my teacher last year. I liked him, but he gave us a lot of homework.

John: He gives us a lot of homework, too. Oh, here's the bus. Maybe I won't be late!

B Circle the verbs in each sentence. Then write each verb in the correct column. If there is no helping verb, write Ø.

	Helping Verb	Main Verb
1. I'm (studying) English.	'm	studying
2. I came here last year.	Ø	came
3. We're waiting for the bus.		
4. I don't own a car.		
5. Are you taking an English class?		
6. We aren't in the same class.		
7. The class ends at 9:00 p.m.		
8. Do you need a ride home?		

C Look at the underlined words. Decide if each one is a main verb or an adjective.

	Main Verb	Adjective
1. Jo usually <u>drives</u>.	✓	
2. He's a <u>serious</u> student.		
3. He doesn't <u>need</u> a ride home today.		
4. We're very <u>busy</u> with school and work.		
5. Are you <u>married</u>, Mika?		
6. Can we <u>study</u> together sometime?		
7. What time does the bus <u>come</u>?		
8. She's not <u>worried</u> about her classes.		

D On a separate piece of paper, write an eight-line conversation between two strangers waiting for a delayed airline flight. Underline the main verbs and circle the helping verbs.

11

Adjectives and Adverbs

Adjectives describe nouns.   Adverbs describe verbs.

She is a **careful** driver.   She drives **carefully**.

Adjectives come after the verb **BE** and before nouns.
You are **careful**.   You are a **careful** driver.

Don't put an adverb between a verb and a noun.

Correct	**Incorrect**
verb noun adverb	verb adverb noun
He speaks English **clearly**.	~~He speaks clearly English~~.

Many adverbs end in -ly.

Adjectives	**Adverbs**
slow	slowly
careful	carefully
clear	clearly
fluent	fluently

Some adverbs look the same as adjectives.

BE + Adjectives	**Adverbs**
They're **hard** workers.	They work **hard**.
They're **early**.	They arrive **early**.
They're **late**.	They arrive **late**.
They're **fast** learners.	They learn **fast**.

Be careful with **well** and **good**.
Well is the adverb form of **good**.
Well is an adjective when it means "not sick."

Adjectives	**Adverbs**
His English is **good**.	He speaks English **well**.
She's not sick. She's **well**.	She is sleeping **well**.

A Read the job advertisements. Circle the correct word from each pair of choices. Then listen to check your answers.

HELP WANTED

Babysitter We need a babysitter to pick up our daughter from school. We want someone who has a car and drives (1. careful/*carefully*).
Call Linda at 555-2054.

Receptionist We need someone who speaks English (2. good/well). Many of our customers are from other countries, so we want someone

who can speak (3. slow/slowly) and (4. clear/clearly).
Call Peter at 555-3752.

Secretary We need someone who can speak English (5. fluent/fluently). We want a (6. fast/fastly) worker who can work (7. good/well) with other people. We want someone who types (8. fast/fastly)—at least 70 words per minute. Call Mike at 555-2303.

B Write the seven adverbs from Exercise A below. Next to each one, write the verb it describes.

Adverb	Verb		Adverb	Verb
1. _carefully_	_drives_	**5.**		
2.		**6.**		
3.		**7.**		
4.				

Which word from Exercise A is an adjective? _____

What word does it describe? _____

C Imagine that you are at a job interview and you say the sentences below. Add an adjective or adverb to complete each sentence.

1. I work _hard_____.

2. I speak English _____.

3. I am a _____ worker.

4. I can learn a new job _____.

5. I'm very _____.

6. I understand English _____.

7. I'm a very _____ person.

D Find the mistakes. Make the corrections.

1. He works ~~good~~ well.

4. Do you speak fluently English?

2. He does well his homework.

5. We work hardly every day.

3. I am a worker good.

6. She holds the baby careful.

E Chant

Fast Learner

He's a fast learner.
He learns very fast.
In his English class,
He's first, not last.

His English is good.
He speaks very well.

He reads and writes,
And he knows how to spell.

His teacher is smart.
Her lessons are great.
The students work hard,
And they're never late.

Prepositions

Prepositions show time, place, movement, and other relationships between words.

Time	Place
The meeting is **at** 7:00 p.m. The meeting is **from** 7:00 **to** 9:00 p.m. I was there **for** three hours. I went **on** Tuesday/**on** April 5th/**in** April.	She lives **on** the second floor. I'm **in** the car. It's **at** school.

Movement	Other
We need to go **to** the meeting. I drove **from** my office **to** the meeting. He drove **through** the tunnel. He went **around** the corner. He drove **over** the bridge. He walked **across** the bridge.	I heard (the news) **about** the accident. It's **on** the radio. It's **on** TV. I need a piece **of** paper. Please come **with** me. I'm **on** the phone. I'm **on** my cell phone.

Some prepositions follow certain words.

I'm worried **about** you.   I arrived **in** New York.

I waited **for** you.   I arrived **at** 7:00 p.m.

A Read the telephone conversation between Joe and his wife Anna. Complete each sentence with a preposition. Then listen to check your answers.

See Appendix H for prepositions of time and place. See Appendix I for phrases with prepositions.

Anna: Joe! Where are you? I'm so worried (1.) _____about_____ you. I heard

the news (2.) _____ the accident (3.) _____ the radio.

Joe: I'm fine, but the traffic isn't moving.

Anna: I heard that a truck went (4.) _____ the tunnel in the

wrong direction and hit a lot of cars.

Joe: That's right. I was driving (5.) _____ the bridge when the

accident happened.

Anna: I'm glad you're OK. Listen, we have a meeting (6.) _____

Amy's teacher (7.) _____ 7 o'clock.

Joe: I know. Can you go (8.) _____ the meeting without me?

Anna: OK, but maybe you can come later. It's (9.) _____ Room . . .

Joe: Wait. I need to find a piece (10.) _____ paper. OK. Go ahead.

Anna: It's in Room 252. It's (11.) _____ the second floor of Building E.

Joe: And what's the name (12.) _____ Amy's teacher? I forgot!

B Write the missing prepositions in the sentences. Then write **T** (time), **P** (place), **M** (movement) or **O** (other) in the space to the left of each sentence.

1. _P_ I'm still __in__ the car.
2. ___ The meeting starts _____ 7:00.
3. ___ We need to go _____ the meeting.
4. ___ I don't want to miss the meeting _____ the teacher.
5. ___ It was impossible to get _____ the tunnel.
6. ___ Nobody could get _____ the bridge.
7. ___ His wife heard the news _____ the radio.
8. ___ He wrote the room number on a piece _____ paper.

C Look at the map of Joe's route. Complete the sentences with a preposition from the box below. Use **in** twice.

in	from	to	around	through	over	at

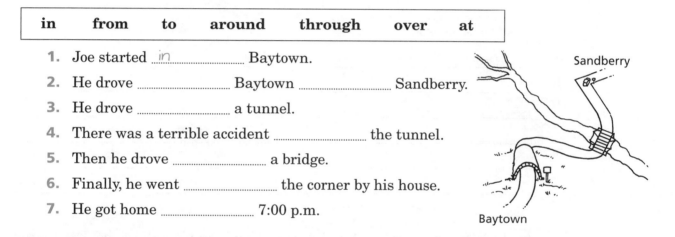

1. Joe started __in__ Baytown.
2. He drove _____ Baytown _____ Sandberry.
3. He drove _____ a tunnel.
4. There was a terrible accident _____ the tunnel.
5. Then he drove _____ a bridge.
6. Finally, he went _____ the corner by his house.
7. He got home _____ 7:00 p.m.

Sandberry

Baytown

D Read the paragraph and circle the prepositions. On a separate piece of paper, write a paragraph about a trip you took and circle the prepositions. Share your paragraph with a partner.

Last year I took a trip (with) my grandfather. We got up really early in the morning and drove six hours from our farm to Iowa City. We didn't stay on the highway. We drove on country roads and went over some beautiful, old one-lane bridges. There was nothing on the radio, so I was glad we had some CDs. We listened to a lot of country music during the trip. When we arrived in Iowa City, we weren't happy about the traffic and noise, but we stayed at my aunt's house for five days and had a good time.

Review

Parts of Speech: Nouns, Verbs, Adjectives, Adverbs, Prepositions

A Dictation Listen to the paragraph about Melissa's job. Write what you hear. Key words: *alphabet, stories, behave, necessary*

Melissa works

....

....

....

....

....

B Look at your paragraph in Exercise A and complete the chart. Don't write the same word more than once, and don't write pronouns.

PARTS OF SPEECH				
Nouns	**Verbs**	**Adjectives**	**Adverbs**	**Prepositions**
Melissa	works	six	early	with

C Find the mistakes in these sentences about kindergartners Johnny and Carol. Make the corrections.

1. Johnny is ᵃ smart little boy.

2. He's a smart.

3. Johnny is an boy athletic.

4. Johnny and his twin sister Carol are intelligents.

5. They excited about school.

6. Carol draws careful.

7. She also sings beautiful.

8. They write their names good.

9. She has two book about dogs.

10. They are in school at 9 a.m. to 3 p.m.

11. Their classroom is in the second floor.

12. They are children very happy.

D Complete this story about Melissa's first day teaching kindergarten. Use the past tense in 5 and 6. More than one answer is possible.

School started (1. preposition) .... on .... September 8th. Melissa was

very (2. adjective) .... because she wanted to do (3. adverb for

good) .... She wanted the (4. noun) .... to like her.

When she (5. verb) .... the children, she (6. verb)

.... and said, "Hi everyone. Welcome to kindergarten. My

(7. noun) .... is Melissa and I am your (8. noun) ...."

When he heard this, a/an (9. adjective) ....

(10. noun) .... walked (11. preposition) .... the door

very (12. adverb) .... He said, "I (13. verb) .... to go

home!" Melissa went to him and said, "(14.) ...."

See Appendix A for
a list of irregular
verbs. See
Appendices H and I
for prepositions.

Have Fun

A **Word Search** Complete the chart. Use your dictionary if necessary. Then, in the puzzle below, find and circle each word that you added to the chart. The words can be vertical (|), horizontal (—), or diagonal (/) (\ ). The words can also be spelled backwards.

Noun	Verb	Adjective	Adverb
beauty	——	beautiful	
a teacher		——	——
an assignment		——	——
	announce	——	——
comfort	comfort		comfortably
a crowd	crowd		——
	excite	excited/exciting	excitedly
a winner		——	——
a decision		decisive	decisively
an owner		——	——
——	——	busy	
	marry	married	——
the beginning		——	——
hunger	——		hungrily
——	——	nervous	

```
H  U  N  G  R  Y  C  R  O  W  D  E  D  J  E
J  N  B  A  N  N  O  U  N  C  E  M  E  N  T
B  E  O  E  R  J  A  W  O  X  A  M  E  N  D
B  E  T  Z  G  Z  L  N  W  E  Y  Q  B  E  W
E  X  J  W  Y  I  G  R  O  W  N  A  C  Z  E
A  C  Q  B  W  V  N  Q  E  X  L  I  G  V  T
U  I  E  P  C  F  U  N  H  N  D  G  T  V  C
T  T  B  U  S  I  L  Y  M  E  N  A  C  B  R
I  E  E  D  R  F  L  A  E  Y  R  I  H  N  P
F  M  C  H  D  D  R  B  R  P  S  W  W  U  G
U  E  K  Y  O  R  B  N  D  B  L  E  M  M  E
L  N  L  M  I  H  T  N  G  I  S  S  A  K  S
L  T  L  A  C  O  M  F  O  R  T  A  B  L  E
Y  O  G  H  C  A  E  T  K  K  E  V  R  V  Y
D  E  P  T  U  Z  N  E  R  V  O  U  S  L  Y
```

B Word Game Join a team of three or four students. Your team will have five minutes to make as many nouns, verbs, and prepositions as you can using the letters in the box. The letters can be used more than once. The team with the most words wins.

B	A	D	I
E	R	U	L
T	S	C	O
M	N	P	F

Nouns	Verbs	Prepositions
sun		

C Chant

Nice Old Cheap Hotel

We found a cheap hotel by the sea.
The breakfast is delicious, and the coffee is free.
The rooms are enormous, but the bathrooms are small.
There's no place to hang the big beach towels at all.

The restaurant is outside under a tree,
And the cook prepares dinner very carefully.
The coffee shop stays open all night,
And you can bring your dog. That's all right.

The tennis courts are fine,
And the swimming pool is great.
We swim there every morning
And never arrive late.

It's perfect for kids. It's perfect for me.
It's a nice old cheap hotel by the sea.

Subjects and Verbs

A sentence has a subject and a verb.

The subject of a sentence can be a noun or a subject pronoun. It is usually the first noun or subject pronoun in the sentence. It often tells who or what is doing something.

Subject	Verb	
Toronto	is	in Canada.
This	is	my sister.
She	lives	in Toronto.

Use subject pronouns to talk about people and things without giving their names.

Singular	Plural
I, you, he, she, it	we, you, they
this, that	these, those

Language Notes:
Don't use a noun and a subject pronoun together.

Correct	Incorrect
Sam works in a factory.	Sam he works in a factory.

Don't omit the subject in a sentence.

Correct	Incorrect
It's very beautiful.	Is very beautiful.

Don't omit the verb in a sentence.

Correct	Incorrect
She's 10 years old.	She 10 years old.

A Listen and read as Sandra talks about photos of her family. Then write **S** over the subjects and underline the verbs.

     S

    This <u>is</u> my sister May. She lives with my parents in Toronto. I don't see her very often. We send email to each other every day. She works in a hospital as a nurse. It's a very good job. But it's not easy.

    And these are my grandparents. They came to Canada many years ago. They don't speak English well. Life in Toronto is difficult for them.

B Sandra is talking about another photo. Read the description below and add the subject (a noun or a pronoun) to each sentence. Then circle the verbs in the sentences.

(1.) _This_ (is) my brother, Li. (2.) .... lives in California. (3.) ....'s married. His wife's name is Karen. (4.) .... comes from Mexico. My brother and his wife are very happy. (5.) .... have a beautiful daughter. (6.) .... is almost a year old. (7.) ....'s her birthday next week.

C Identify the problem in each sentence. Make the corrections.

	No Subject	No Verb	Two Subjects
1. It ̶I̶s̶ hot today.	✓	....	....
2. My parents they live in New York.	....	....	....
3. My sister she has a job at a bank.	....	....	....
4. She happy.	....	....	....
5. Is a very good job.	....	....	....
6. This my brother.	....	....	....
7. These my parents.	....	....	....

D Bring in a photo or draw a picture of a friend or family member. Write a paragraph about the person. Use the paragraph in Exercise B as a model. Underline the subjects and circle the verbs.

Possible first sentence: This is my best friend Tina.

LESSON 7

And, Or, But, So, Because

Use **and**, **or**, **but**, **so**, and **because** to connect two sentences.

Sentence		Sentence
He's nice to me,	and	he gives me presents.
Is she in love with Mark,	or	is she in love with John?
He's handsome,	but	he's not very nice to me.
She needed advice,	so	she wrote to *Dear Annie*.
She wrote to *Dear Annie*	because	she needed advice.

Use **and**, **or**, and **but** to connect nouns with nouns, verbs with verbs, adjectives with adjectives, and adverbs with adverbs.

Two nouns:	Mark and John are her two boyfriends.
Three verbs:	He called me, took me to a restaurant, and brought me flowers.
Two adjectives:	Was the restaurant expensive or inexpensive?
Two adverbs:	He talks romantically but not honestly.

Comma Rules:

- Use a comma before **and**, **or**, **but**, and **so** when they connect two sentences.
- When **and**, **but**, or **or** connect three or more words or groups of words, use commas to separate the words.
  He says I'm beautiful, smart, and funny.
- When **because** comes in the middle of a sentence, don't add a comma.

Don't omit the subject after **because**.

Correct	**Incorrect**
I like him because he's kind to me.	~~I like him because is kind to me.~~

A sentence has a subject and a verb.

A Read the letter to the advice column *Dear Annie*. Write **and**, **or**, **but**, **so**, or **because** in each space. Then listen to check your answers.

Dear Annie,

   I have a problem. I have two boyfriends, Mark (1.) *and* John. Mark is handsome, (2.) _____ he isn't very nice to me. For example, last week I got angry at him (3.) _____ he didn't remember my birthday.

   My other boyfriend is John. He isn't very handsome, (4.) _____ he is very kind to me. Last week he called me, took me to an expensive restaurant, (5.) _____ sent me flowers. I like him a lot, (6.) _____ I'm really in love with Mark.

   Last week both Mark (7.) _____ John invited me to the senior dance. Should I go with Mark (8.) _____ John?

   Confused

22

B Read the sentences. Add commas where necessary. Then write the connecting words and what is being connected (nouns, verbs, adjectives, or sentences).

	Connecting Word	What is Being Connected
1. I have two boyfriends, Mark and John.	and	nouns
2. Mark is handsome but he isn't nice to me.		
3. He didn't call me or send me a present.		
4. He didn't call me because he was busy.		
5. He didn't call me so I got angry at him.		
6. I'm beautiful smart and funny.		
7. Should I go to the dance or stay home?		
8. Should I go with Mark or John?		
9. I can't decide so I'll probably stay home.		

C As a class, talk about what *Confused* should do: stay with Mark, stay with John, or leave them both. Then find a partner who agrees with you and write a letter to *Confused*. Include sentences with **and**, **or**, **but**, **so**, and **because**.

Dear Confused,

We are writing to give you advice about your boyfriends. We think you should

Good luck to you!

_____ and _____

LESSON 8

BE—Present/Past/Future (with *Will*)

The verb **BE** has six forms.

Future:
will (won't) be

Past:
was (wasn't), were (weren't)

Present:
am (am not), is (isn't), are (aren't)

Use **BE** before nouns, adjectives, and prepositional phrases.

Noun	**Adjective**	**Prepositional Phrase**
He'll **be** a *singer*.	His life **was** *difficult*.	He's *from Mexico*.

Yes-No Questions

Present and Past Tenses
Move the verb **BE** (am, is, are, was, were) to the *front* of the sentence.
Put the subject right after **BE**.

	BE	**Subject**		
Correct:	Was	his life	difficult?	**Incorrect:** ~~Was difficult his life?~~

Future Tense with will
Put the subject between **Will** and **be**. Don't omit **be**.

Correct:	Will he **be** famous?	**Incorrect:** ~~Will he famous?~~

Use **BE** with age and the word **born**. He **is** 32. He **was** born in Mexico.

A Mylo, a famous rock musician, is being interviewed. Complete the sentences with a subject and a form of the verb **BE**. Then listen to check your answers.

Interviewer: So Mylo, tell me about your childhood. (1.) __Were you__ born in Mexico City?

Mylo: No, (2.) _____. (3.) _____ born in a small village.

Interviewer: (4.) _____ interested in music as a child?

Mylo: Yes. I started to play the guitar when (5.) _____ eight.

Interviewer: Wow! (6.) _____ young! Tell me about your life now.

Mylo: Well, (7.) _____ married now. My wife and I have a daughter. (8.) _____ two next week.

Interviewer: Congratulations! And what are your future plans?

Mylo: Well, (9.) _____ in Europe next month.

Interviewer: (10.) .... in Miami again soon?

Mylo: No, I'm sorry, (11.) ....

Interviewer: That's too bad for us. Well, good luck on your tour!

B Write the verb tense of each sentence (past, present or future). Then look at the underlined words. Write **noun**, **adjective**, or **prepositional phrase** (*PP*).

		Verb Tense	Words after *BE*
1.	My parents were <u>farmers</u>.	past	noun
2.	I was <u>happy</u> to practice the guitar.		
3.	My daughter will be a <u>musician</u>.		
4.	Your new song is <u>popular</u>.		
5.	You're a very famous <u>singer</u>.		
6.	My wife won't be in <u>Europe</u> next month.		
7.	I'll be <u>at your next concert</u>.		

C Laura Gee is another popular singer. Look at the information below. On a separate piece of paper, write ten **yes-no** questions and short answers about Laura.

EXAMPLE: Was Laura born in 1985?

Laura Gee's Life		
In the 80s	**Now**	**Next month**
born–1985: Argentina	very exciting life	trip to Asia
shy, sweet	very popular songs	
mother–doctor	husband–American actor	**Next year**
father–doctor	parents–retired	first movie

D Chant

Getting to Know You

Were you interested in sports
when you were in school?
    Yes, I was.
    I was always in the pool.
I was a pretty good swimmer.
    I was too!

But I'm a sailor now.
    I am too!
What are your plans?
Will you be here in June?
    No, I'll be in Hawaii.
    On my honeymoon.

Present Tense with *When, Before,* and *After*

See the inside back cover for -s spelling rules.

Use the present tense to talk about something that repeats or is routine.

Add **-s** to verbs after **he, she,** and **it.**

Affirmative		**Negative**	
I/You/We/They	work.	I/You/We/They	don't work.
He/She/It	works.	He/She/It	doesn't work.

Connect two sentences with **when, before,** or **after** to describe when something happens.

When has three meanings:

- at the same time: He listens to the radio when he washes the dishes.
- (=*while*)   When he washes the dishes, he listens to the radio.*
- every time: I call my mother when I'm homesick.
- (=*whenever*)   When I'm homesick, I call my mother.*
- right after: He has a snack when he gets home.
   When he gets home, he has a snack.*

Before and After

5:30	5:35	5:45	7:00	8:00
He gets home.	He has a snack.	He studies.	He eats dinner.	He reads.

He eats dinner before he reads.   OR   Before he reads, he eats dinner.*

He studies after he has a snack.   OR   After he has a snack, he studies.*

*Use a comma when a sentence starts with **When, Before,** or **After.**

A Write the verbs in the present tense. Then listen to Linda talk about a typical evening at her house. Circle **T** for *True* or **F** for *False.*

1. (walk)   My son Mark ___walks___ home from school.   T   (F)

2. (arrive)   The bus _____ at 6:00 p.m.   T   F

3. (cook)   I _____ dinner when we get home.   T   F

4. (study)   Mark _____ when he   T   F

5. (get)   _____ home.

6. (play)   Mark _____ computer games.   T   F

7. (have)   My husband Charlie _____ coffee   T   F

8. (come)   when _____ he home.

9. (relax)   He _____ on the couch.   T   F

10. (wash)   I _____ the dishes after we eat.   T   F

11. (do)   My son _____ his homework   T   F

12. (go)   before he _____ to bed.

B Make the false sentences from Exercise A negative and write them below. Then listen again and write the correct information. Change **my** to **your**. Change **I** to **you**.

1. Mark doesn't walk home from school. He takes the bus.

2.

3.

4.

5.

C Look at these pictures of Charlie's evening routine. On a separate piece of paper, write six sentences using **when**, **before**, and **after**. Put these words at the beginning of three sentences and in the middle of the three other sentences.

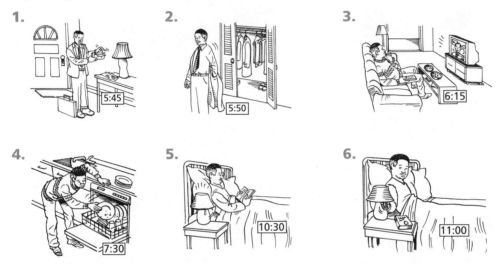

D Write short answers to these questions about yourself. Then ask two students the same questions. Take notes in the chart. On a separate piece of paper, write eight sentences about you and your classmates.

Question	You	Student 1	Student 2
What do you do after you finish class?			
What do you do before you go to bed?			
What do you do when you're bored?			
What do you do when you have a cold?			

<table>
<tr><td>

Lessons

6–9</td><td>

Review

Subjects and Verbs
And, Or, But, So, Because, BE
Present Tense with *When/Before/After*</td></tr>
</table>

 A Dictation Listen to the paragraph about Mike's annual visit to the doctor. Write what you hear. Then circle the subjects and underline the verbs. Most of the sentences have more than one subject and verb.
Key words: *check-up, junk food, couch potato*

Mike doesn't want

....

....

....

....

....

....

....

B Mike is now a member of an exercise club. Complete the sentences with a word from the box. More than one answer is possible, and words can be used more than once.

and	but	or	so	because	before	when	after

Mike has a new life (1.) _because_ he exercises every day. His doctor told him he has high blood pressure, (2.) _____ he wants to improve his health. Now he feels better (3.) _____ he has more energy.

(4.) _____ he goes to the gym, he lifts weights for a half hour (5.) _____ he uses the treadmill for the same amount of time. He takes a shower (6.) _____ he's done, and then he goes home to walk the dog. Then he eats out, (7.) _____ he eats at home. He doesn't eat junk food anymore, (8.) _____ sometimes he misses it.

(9.) _____ he changed his lifestyle, he had high blood pressure (10.) _____ other health problems (11.) _____ he didn't take care of himself. Now he's a new man!

C Find the mistakes in these sentences about Mike. Make the corrections.

                was
1. Mike born in Vancouver.
2. He 25 years old.
3. Mike he exercises a lot.
4. He goes to the gym a lot. Is very energetic.
5. He eats well because wants to be healthy.
6. He will very healthy.
7. He will have normal blood pressure?
8. He won't a couch potato anymore.
9. He isn't careful about his health in the past.
10. Whenever he get exercise, he feels good.
11. He don't like to eat junk food now.
12. At the gym, lifts weights, uses the treadmill, and takes a shower.

D On a separate piece of paper, write a paragraph about yourself and your family. Write affirmative and negative sentences. Use **BE** in the present, past, and future tenses.

Examples of language you can use:

BE + Adjectives	BE + Nouns	BE + Prepositional Phrases
shy	a high school student	from Mexico
hardworking	a babysitter	on time
easy	a good mother/father	in love
interested in ___	an athlete	on vacation
late for class	a chef	with my wife/friend
worried about ___		
married		

EXAMPLE:

    I was born in Minnesota in 1960. I'm a chef at a French restaurant, and I'm very happy there. My daughter is a high school student. Unfortunately, she's in love now, so she isn't very interested in school. My son is ten years old. He's a very good athlete. We will be on vacation next month in Mexico or Brazil. We won't be home until August.

Have Fun

A Crossword Puzzle

Across

3. She doesn't .... a lot of time with her family.

6. She gives me good advice, ... I tell her everything.

7. She's rich, famous, and ....

9. She .... three movies a year.

10. I visit her .... I'm in L.A.

11. She's American, ... she was born in London.

Down

1. My best friend .... born in London.

2. These .... some pictures of her.

4. She .... work in the summer.

5. She can tell me anything .... she knows I can keep a secret.

7. Will she .... in London next month?

8. Now she .... in L.A.

10. She .... be at the party because she'll be in Africa.

B **Guessing Game** Write three true and one false present tense sentence about your routines: things you do every day, every weekend, or every summer. Use **before**, **when**, **after**, and **because**. Your classmates will guess which sentence is false.

EXAMPLE: You: *Every summer, I go camping because I love nature. Before I go camping, I pack my tent and other supplies. After I get to the campground, I take a lot of hikes. I'm always very dirty when I get back home.*

Your classmate: *You don't take hikes. You just relax!*

You: *No, you're wrong. I love to take hikes when I'm in nice places.*

Another classmate: *You don't pack a tent.*

You: *That's right! I don't pack my tent. I don't have a tent. I'm pretty lucky because my friend has all the supplies.*

C **Chant**

Success Story

She's not very nice,
but she'll be a success.

She knows how to talk,
And she knows how to dress.

She always has a meeting before she goes home,
And she makes a few calls on her new cell phone.

She loves big cities.
She was born in L.A.

Her boss really likes her.
He thinks she's OK.

Her boss really likes her.
He thinks she's OK.

She loves big cities.
She was born in L.A.

Contrast: Present and Present Continuous Tenses

See Appendix C for more time expressions.

Use the present tense to talk about something that repeats or is a routine. He always **makes** noise. They **don't listen** to me. **Does** he usually **practice** at night? Why **do** they **practice** at night?	Use the present continuous tense to talk about what is happening right now or a future plan. He's **making** noise right now. They **aren't listening** to me. **Is** he **practicing** tonight? Why **are** they **practicing** now?

Time Expressions

Present Tense	**Present Continuous Tense**
• every: minute, hour, day, week, month, year • frequency adverbs: always, almost always, usually, often, sometimes, rarely, never • on Mondays • once a day, twice a week	• now, right now • these days • today, tomorrow, at noon, at 6:00 • this: morning, afternoon, weekend

Language Notes:

• The verb **live** means the same thing in the present or present continuous tense.

    Janet **lives** in Vancouver.   Janet **is living** in Vancouver.

• Frequency adverbs usually come between the subject and the verb. Other time expressions usually come at the beginning or end of a sentence.

Correct: They **always** make noise.   **Incorrect:** ~~Always they make noise.~~

Correct: He plays in a band **twice a week**.   **Incorrect:** ~~He plays twice a week in a band.~~

A Read the phone conversation between Janet and Lynn. Circle the correct choice in each pair. Listen to the conversation to check your answers.

Lynn: Hi, Janet. What (1. are you doing/do you do) right now?

Janet: Well, I (2. 'm trying/try) to write my essay, but I can't concentrate. My neighbor (3. is playing/plays) loud music. Can you hear it?

Lynn: Yes! That's terrible. (4. Is he always making/Does he always make) so much noise?

Janet: Yes. He (5. is playing/plays) in a band once a week. He and his friends (6. are practicing/practice) every night, and I'm getting tired of it. So, what (7. are you doing/do you do) now? Do you want to meet me at Biff's Café?

Lynn: Sure!

B Lynn and Janet are at the door of Biff's Café. Complete each sentence with the correct form of the verb in parentheses. Use the present or the present continuous tense.

Lynn: What's going on? Biff's is so crowded! Whenever I

(1. come) come _____ here, it's empty.

Janet: Look! That's Mylo, the famous rock star! He (2. play)

_____ his guitar!

Lynn: You're kidding! I can't believe Mylo (3. perform)

_____ here.

Janet: He (4. give) _____ surprise free concerts when

he (5. travel) _____. Listen, he (6. sing)

_____ my favorite song.

Lynn: It's hard to hear.

Janet: Some people (7. dance) _____.

Lynn: Really? Where? There's no place to dance.

Janet: Look! Someone (8. come) _____ to the door.

Lynn: What's he saying?

Janet: Mylo (9. play) _____ tomorrow night again! He

(10. give) _____ free tickets!

C Lynn and Janet are at a fair. With a partner, describe the scene on a separate piece of paper. Write four sentences in the present tense and four sentences in the present continuous tense. Use at least three time expressions.

Example first sentence: *Every year, Janet and Lynn go to the fair.*

Non-Action Verbs

Non-action verbs are not usually used in the present continuous tense. Use these verbs in the present tense to talk about what is happening right now.

Senses	Feelings	Opinion	Possession	Mental States	Other
hear	feel	agree	belong	forget	be
look	hate	believe	have	know	cost
see	like	disagree	own	remember	mean
smell	love	feel		understand	need
sound		think			owe
taste					want

Correct	Incorrect
She likes her class.	She's liking her class.
I don't understand.	I'm not understanding.

Have and **think** can be non-action verbs and action verbs.

Non-Action (present)	Action (present continuous)
Have (possession):	Have (not possession):
I have a lot of homework.	I'm having a good time. I'm having fun.
He doesn't have time today.	He's having trouble. We aren't having lunch.
Think (belief/opinion):	Think:
I think that math is hard.	I'm thinking about dropping my class.

See, look, smell, and taste can also be non-action or action verbs.

A Read the email from Paula to her mother. Circle the correct choice in each of the sentences. Then listen to check your answers.

To: Ellen Wong	From: Paula Wong

Dear Mom,

Hi! I hope all is well. School is OK. As you know, (1. I take/**I'm taking**) three classes: English, art, and math. (2. I like/I'm liking) the art and English classes, but (3. I have/I'm having) trouble with my math class. The teacher (4. knows/is knowing) that the class is difficult for me. (5. She often helps me/She's often helping) me with my homework after class, but (6. I still don't understand/I'm still not understanding) it. In fact, (7. I think about/I'm thinking about) dropping my math class.

Mom, please understand. (8. I have/I'm having) a lot of homework in my other classes. (9. I want/I'm wanting) to get good grades at school, so (10. I really think/I'm really thinking) that I should drop the class. Please don't be angry!

Love, Paula

B Find the verbs below in Exercise A. Write the form of the verb in the first column. Then decide whether the verb is a non-action or an action verb.

BASE FORM	Form in Exercise A	Non-Action Verb	Action Verb
1. take	'm taking		✓
2. have			
3. know			
4. understand			
5. think about			
6. have			
7. think that			

C Complete the conversation between Paula's parents by writing the correct form of the verbs in parentheses. Use the present or present continuous tense.

Jan: I got an email from Paula today. She (1. [not] do) ___'s not doing___
well in her math class and she (2. want) _____ to drop it.
She (3. [not] need) _____ math because she
(4. study) _____ art. And she (5. take) _____
two other classes now. That's a lot with her part-time job.

do well = do a good
job

Ken: Well, I (6. think) _____ that math is very important.
She (7. need) _____ to stay in her math class.

Jan: I'm sorry, Dan. I (8. [not] agree) _____ with you about
this. Let's talk about it more tomorrow.

D Chant

Dinner for Two

I have a headache.
  I do too.
My relatives are here.
  Mine are too.
I don't want to cook.
  Neither do I.
But they hate to eat in restaurants.
I don't know why.

I love to cook.
  I do too.
But I like small parties,
Dinner for two.
    That sounds very good to me,
    Dinner for two.
I agree.

LESSON 12

Past Tense

To form the past tense, add **-ed** or **-d** to regular verbs.

Present
He travels to Vietnam every year.
He visits his family.

Past
He traveled there last month.
He visited his family.

Many verbs are irregular. They do not end in **-ed**.

Base form:	come	buy	catch	do	fall	go	have	make
Past form:	came	bought	caught	did	fell	went	had	made

Use **didn't (did not)** + the base form to make regular and irregular verbs negative.

	Affirmative	**Negative**
Regular Verb:	He missed the plane.	He didn't miss the plane.
Irregular Verb:	We bought a ticket.	We didn't buy a ticket.

Language Notes:
- Do not add **-ed** to verbs after **to**.
  Correct: He wanted to stay. **Incorrect:** He wanted to stayed.
- Do not add **-ed** to the base forms of verbs in negatives and questions.
  Correct: He didn't miss the plane. **Incorrect:** He didn't missed the plane.
- The past form of a verb is the same for all subjects: I/you/he/she/we/they went.

- Use the past tense with words like **then**, **after a while**, and **finally** to describe the order of events or tell a story.

A Listen and read along as Sam talks about his trip to Vietnam. Underline the irregular past tense verbs. Then, on a separate piece of paper, write the irregular past tense verbs in their base and past tense forms. Write **be** only once.

Last year, I decided to go to Vietnam to visit my family. I <u>made</u> my reservation and bought my ticket online. I was very excited about my trip.

The day of my trip was terrible. First, I almost missed the plane because the taxi came to my house 30 minutes late. Then I had to stand in line and go through security. I was in such a hurry that I left one of my bags on the floor. A nice woman ran after me and gave me my bag. Finally, I found the right gate. When I got to my seat, I sat down, read the newspaper, and fell asleep.

B Circle **T** for **True** or **F** for **False** next to each sentence about Sam's trip. If a sentence is false, make it negative. If a sentence is true, write, "That's true," and add extra information.

1. (T) F   Last year Sam went to Vietnam.
   That's true. Last year Sam went to Vietnam.

2. T F   He used a computer to buy his ticket.

3. T F   He missed the plane.

4. T F   He took the bus to the airport.

5. T F   He left his bag on the bus.

6. T F   A woman gave him his bag.

C Complete the story using past tense verbs. More than one answer is possible.

My wife and I (1.) _____came_____ to the United States ten years ago. At that time, the economic situation in my country was very bad. I (2. not) _____ a good job.

When we (3.) _____ here, our life was very difficult. We (4. not) _____ much English. I (5.) _____ a job as a carpenter, and my wife (6.) _____ an English course. After a while, we (7.) _____ money and (8.) _____ to California.

D Write six sentences about a trip you took to a new place. Try to use **then**, **after a while**, and **finally**.

FIRST SENTENCE:

_____ _went to_ _____ _____.
        name(s)   place   ___ ago

13

Used To

Use **used to** + the base form of a verb to talk about a past habit or custom.

Use or **used** are both possible as the main verb in questions and negatives.

Affirmative Statements

Life **used to** be easier. = In the past, life was easier.
Girls **used to** wear skirts every day. = In the past, girls wore skirts every day.
Gasoline **used to** cost 25 cents a gallon. = In the past, gasoline cost 25 cents a gallon.

Negative Statements

I **never used to/didn't used to** get sick. = In the past, I didn't get sick.
Never used to is more common than **didn't use to**.

Yes-No Questions

Did you **use to** have long hair? = Did you have long hair in the past?
Did you **used to** be shy? = Were you shy in the past?

Language Note:
• Don't use the **-ing** form of the verb with **used to**.
Correct: I used to live with my uncle. **Incorrect:** ~~I used to living with my uncle.~~

A Sylvia is taking her grandson Bob to the movies and explaining how life used to be in the United States. Complete the conversation by filling in each space with **used to** and a verb from the box. Then listen to check your answers.

wait in line	be	ride	buy	come	deliver	go

Sylvia: I need to get some cash. Let's stop at the ATM. You know, Bob, when I was young, we didn't have ATMs. We (1.) _____ at the bank to withdraw money.

Bob: Really?

Sylvia: Yes. I remember that I (2.) _____ to the bank during my lunch hour. Sometimes I didn't have time for lunch!

Bob: So, do you think things are easier now, Grandma?

Sylvia: Well, I think in many ways, life (3.) _____ easier. For example, when I was a child, we never (4.) _____ milk in the grocery store. The milkman (5.) _____ milk to our house. And when we were sick, the doctor (6.) _____ to our house, too. We didn't have to drive to the doctor's office.

Bob: Wow! Did you (7.) .... a horse to school, too?

Sylvia: Come on, Bob! I'm not *that* old!

B Rewrite these sentences and questions about the past. Use **used to** and the base form of the verb.

1. In the 1950s, gas in the United States cost only 25 cents a gallon.

   In the 1950s, gas used to cost only 25 cents a gallon.

2. In the1960s, many men had long hair in the United States.

   ....

3. A long time ago, people thought that the world was flat.

   ....

4. Did people think that men lived on Mars?

   ....

5. More people smoked cigarettes 50 years ago.

   ....

6. Doctors made house calls many years ago, but now people have to go to the doctor.

   ....

7. Women didn't wear pants before the 1920s.

   ....

8. Did women in the U.S. have the right to vote in the 1800s?

   ....

9. People had a lot of children to help them do the work on farms.

   ....

10. A long time ago, people never cooked with artificial ingredients.

    ....

C Read the paragraph below about childhood memories. Underline the verbs with **used to**. Then, on a separate piece of paper, write a similar paragraph about yourself. Share your paragraph with a partner or group.

When I was a child, I had an easy life. I never <u>used to work</u> very hard. I used to walk a short distance to school every morning. After school, my friends and I used to stop at the candy store on the way home. Then we used to play games outside until it got dark. My mother used to just shout my name when it was time for dinner. Yes, my life used to be very easy.

Review

Present vs. Present Continuous, Non-Action Verbs, Past Tense, *Used To*

A Dictation Listen to Jennifer talk about her experience at the taping of a TV show. Write what you hear. Then circle the irregular verbs. Key words: *Hollywood, audience, applause signs, experience*

I used to dream

B Jennifer goes to see the taping of a TV show in Hollywood every year. Rewrite the dictation from Exercise A in the present tense.

Every year, I get free tickets to a TV show in Hollywood.

C Complete the conversation with the correct form of the words in parentheses. Use the present or present continuous tense.

Steven: What (1. you/look) _are you looking_ at?

Jennifer: The tickets for the TV show.

Steven: When (2. we/go) _____?

Jennifer: Steven, (3. I/know) _____ (4. you/want) _____ to go, but this year (5. I/feel) _____ like staying home. (6. I/[not] want) _____ to go.

Steven: (7. I/[not] believe) _____ it! What (8. you/say) _____? (9. We/go) _____ every year.

Jennifer: (10. I/[not] have to) _____ go. (11. I/know) _____ the tickets were free, but it's a pain to go in all that L.A. traffic.

Steven: You surprise me. Listen, (12. I/think) _____ that I can change your mind. Will you go if I drive this time?

D Find the mistakes. Make the corrections.

1. ~~Always~~ Jennifer ˄gets free tickets. _(always)_
2. She visits once a year Los Angeles.
3. She didn't wanted to drive.
4. When she goes, she is having a good time.
5. Jennifer and her friend sitting in good seats right now.
6. They are laugh and talk a lot.
7. She is liking to do this because it's free and fun.
8. Two years ago, her best friend didn't went with her because she had a cold.
9. Did she bought the tickets?
10. They wanted to saw famous people in Hollywood.
11. Jennifer's friend used to thinking about a career in acting.
12. Was she go to Hollywood?

LESSONS 10–13

Have Fun

A Unscramble the letters to create regular and irregular past tense verbs. Then use the numbered letters to find the secret message.

SDRUTODNEO   u n d e r s t o o d
      (4)

OHGTUHT

WKNE   (3)

UGORBHT   (8)

DEOR   (7)

OTREW

YEDONJE   (9)

HTUBOG   (10) (2)

LPSTE   (11)

GHCAUT   (12)

AUTTGH

DAPI   (15) (13)

UPT   (14)

ASYEDT   (16) (1)

EOPSK   (6)

SMAW   (5)

WHERT

Secret message boxes:
[ ][ ][ ][ ]' [ ][ ][ ][ ][ ]! [ ][ ] [ ][ ][ ][ ][ ]!
1 2 3 4   5 6 7 8 9   10 11   12 13 14 15 16

42

B **Spelling Bee** Stand in a line. Your teacher will say the base form of a regular or irregular verb. One by one, students will spell the past forms. When students make mistakes, they will sit down. The last student spelling a verb correctly is the winner.

C Chant

The Good Student

Susy took a French class twice a week.
She learned how to write and she learned how to speak.
She used to call her boyfriend every day,
But her old French boyfriend moved away.

Now she's studying Spanish with her new friend Joe.
They're planning a trip to Mexico.
She goes to her class every night at seven.
She has coffee with Joe, and she comes home at eleven.

But she doesn't have time to practice all day.
And it's hard to remember the right words to say.
But she likes her class. She thinks it's fun.
Now she's learning new words one by one.

She learned to say, "My name is Sue."
And now she's practicing, "I love you."

LESSON 14

Future Tense with *Be going to* and *Will*

Future Time Expressions: next week; next month; next year; tomorrow; the day after tomorrow; tonight; in three days; in a little while; on Monday; this weekend

Use **be going to** when you want talk about the future, especially when you are talking about plans.

Subject + BE (+ not)	Going To	Base Form of Main Verb
I'm (not)	going to	call.
You're/They're (not)	going to	go.
He's/She's/It's (not)	going to	come.

To make a **Yes-No** question, move the **BE** verb in front of the subject.

Are you going to call tomorrow?   Is she going to come?

Use **will** to talk about the future, especially when making a prediction.

Subject	Will	Base Form of Main Verb
I/You/He/She/It/We/They	will/won't	win.

To make a **Yes-No** question, move **will** in front of the subject.

Will they be at the birthday party?   Will he call his brother back?

When you're not sure about the future, use

- **(don't) think + will**   I (don't) think that she'll retire.
- **will probably**   We'll probably be busy.
- **probably won't**   We probably won't be home.

A Anne is talking to her husband Charlie. Complete the conversation by filling in each space with **be going to** plus the words in parentheses. Then listen to check your answers.

Anne: Your brother called this morning. (1. you/call) _Are you going to call_ him back?

Charlie: No, (2. I/not call) _____ him. I'm too busy.

Anne: But it's his birthday tomorrow.

Charlie: Oh, you're right!

Anne: (3. you/buy) _____ him a present?

Charlie: Maybe. I think (4. I/get) _____ him a fishing rod. (5. He and Nancy/retire) _____ soon, and I know they both enjoy fishing.

Anne: That's true. You know, we should invite them over for dinner Saturday.

Charlie: Good idea!

Anne: Wait! I forgot. (6. We/not be) _____ home.

Charlie: Why not?

Anne: Remember? It's our anniversary. (7. You/take) _____ me out to dinner!

44

B Change **be going to** to **will**. Change **will** to **be going to**.

be going to	will
1. I'm going to call him back.	....
2.	Will you call him back?
3. We're probably not going to be home.	....
4.	He won't call him back today.
5. Are they going to call him today?	....
6.	She'll call back later.

C Write a **yes-no** question or an answer on each line.

1. Q: ....?

   A: No, Charlie isn't going to call his brother now.

2. Q: ....?

   A: No, his brother won't be at their anniversary dinner.

3. Q: What will Charlie probably get his brother for his birthday?

   A: ....

4. Q: What do you think you will probably do on your next birthday?

   A: ....

5. Q: What probably won't happen on your next birthday?

   A: ....

D Look at Anne's calendar. On a separate piece of paper, write about her plans. Use these time words: **on (a day/date)**, **the day after tomorrow**, **next weekend**, **in two weeks**. (See Appendix C for time expressions.)

- Write five sentences with **be going to** for plans that are certain.
- Write two sentences with **will probably** for less certain plans. (A question mark (?) means the plans are not certain.)
- Write two negative sentences with **be going to**.
- Write two negative sentences with **probably won't**.

FEBRUARY

Monday	Tuesday	Wednesday	Thursday	Friday	Saturday	Sunday
1 TODAY	2	3 go to computer class	4	5	6 celebrate our anniversary	7
8 pick up Jasmine at the airport	9	10 get a haircut	11 buy Valentine's cards?	12	13 take a trip to Atlanta?	14 go to a Valentine's party

45

Future Tense with *Will/Won't* in Different Situations

Use **will** and **won't** + the base form of a verb in different situations.

To make an offer (**will** only)
A: I need help!
B: **I'll** help you.

To refuse (**won't** only)
A: Will you speak at the wedding?
B: No, I **won't**. I'm too shy.

To make a promise
A: Will you be there?
B: Yes, **I'll** be there./Yes, I **will**.*

A: Please don't smoke at the wedding.
B: Don't worry. I **won't**.

*When **will** is the last word in a sentence, don't use a contraction.

To make a prediction
They **will** have a happy marriage.   They probably **won't** have children soon.

• Use **I'm sure** when you're very confident about a prediction.
I'm sure she'll be a good teacher.   **I'm sure** they **won't** wait until they're older.

• Use **I think/I don't think** before the subject + **will** when you are not sure about a prediction.
I think they'll come.   **I don't think** they'll come.

Use **will** with other words to talk about the future.
She **hopes** her daughter **will** be a teacher.   I **know** they **won't** be late.   I **think** I'll go.

A Theresa is talking to her friend Elizabeth about her daughter Emily's wedding. Match what they say to make short conversations. Listen to check your answers.

Theresa
_c_ **1.** Please come to the wedding.
...... **2.** They're getting married, and they're only twenty.
...... **3.** I have so much to do.
...... **4.** We're going to meet his parents tomorrow for lunch.
...... **5.** Please don't tell them that I'm worried.
...... **6.** There are so many invitations to write.

Elizabeth
a. I'll help you. Call any time.
b. Don't worry. I won't.
c. I promise I'll be there.
d. I hope you'll like each other.
e. They love each other very much. I'm sure they'll be happy.
f. I'll write them for you.

Elizabeth
...... **7.** Are you planning to order flowers?
...... **8.** Let me do the invitations for you!
...... **9.** Are they going to go on a honeymoon?
...... **10.** I don't have a car.
...... **11.** Be happy for them! Try to relax!

Theresa
g. OK, I'll try.
h. I'll find someone to give you a ride.
i. Yes, I think I'll buy roses.
j. No, they probably won't. They don't have much money.
k. No, I won't let you! It's too much work.

B Complete the conversation with phrases from the box.

I hope you'll relax	I'll stay	I won't
I hope you'll stay	I'm sure you'll be	I'll help

Theresa: Emily, (1.) *I hope you'll stay* in school.

Emily: Don't worry, Mom. (2.) _____ in school. I
promise! I want to be a teacher. You know that.

Theresa: I know. I just wanted to hear you say it. (3.) _____
a great teacher.

Emily: Well, thanks Mom. (4.) _____. You worry
too much.

Theresa: But that's what mothers do, honey! Anyway, I have to get off the
phone right now to work on the invitations.

Emily: Mom, please let me do the invitations. It's my wedding.

Theresa: No, (5.) _____. I don't mind doing them.

Emily: OK. But (6.) _____ you.

C Write four sentences about an event you are going to in the future. Use **will**
or **won't** in each sentence.

1. _____

2. _____

3. _____

4. _____

D Chant

Party Panic

Will you be at my party?
    Of course I will.
Don't forget the date!
    Of course I won't.
Remember, it's going to be on the first of May.
And the first of May is a week from today!
I hope the food will be all right.
    The food will be fine, and the party's
        not tonight!

I hope the weather won't be bad.
    I can't help you with the weather,
    but don't get mad.
    I'm sure your party will be lots
        of fun
For you, for me, for everyone!

16 Future Tense with Time and *If* Clauses

A clause is a sentence or part of a sentence. It includes a subject and a verb.

     s   v
before she goes = clause

Time clauses can begin with **before**, **when**, or **after**.

Use a time clause to say when something will happen.

If clauses are clauses that begin with **if**.

Use an *if* clause to talk about something that will happen as a result of something else.

A sentence with a time/*if* clause also has a main clause.

Time/*If* clauses can come at the beginning or at the end of a sentence.

Time/If Clause (present tense)	**Main Clause** (future tense)	**Main Clause** (future tense)	**Time/If Clause** (present tense)
Before she goes,	she's going to eat.	She's going to eat	before she goes.
When she's done,	she'll relax.	She'll relax	when she's home.
After she eats,	she'll feel better.	She'll feel better	after she eats.
If I'm nervous,	I won't do well.	I won't do well	if I'm nervous.

Language Notes:

- When the time/*if* clause comes at the beginning of a sentence, add a comma.
- Use the present tense to express future time in the time/*if* clause.
- Use the future tense in the main clause.

Correct: After I finish my work, I will go home.
Incorrect: ~~After I will finish my work, I will go home.~~

 A Read the conversation. Underline the time and *if* clauses. Then listen.

Tom: Are you ready for your job interview?

Alice: I'm so worried about it! <u>If I don't get this job</u>, I'm going to be so disappointed.

Tom: But you're so talented. The interviewer will be very impressed with you when he meets you.

Alice: But I'm so nervous. I don't know what I'm going to say if he asks me about my job experience. I don't have any job experience!

Tom: You're only 16 years old. If he expects a lot of experience, I'll be surprised.

Alice: I guess you're right. I'm going to eat something before I go to the interview.

Tom: OK. After you eat, I'll help you prepare.

B Write the time and *if* clauses from Exercise A below. Put a check (✓) in the center column if there is a comma in the sentence.

	Time/*If* Clause	Comma?	Main Clause
1.	If I don't get this job,	✓	I'm going to be so disappointed.
2.			
3.			

	Main Clause		Time/*If* Clause
4.			
5.			
6.			

C Alice is thinking about her job interview. Complete the time/*if* clauses and main clauses using the correct form of the words in the parentheses.

My job interview is in three hours. Before I (1. leave) _____leave_____, I
(2. practice) _____ for the interview with my brother. I (3. try) _____
to relax when I (4. get) _____ to the office. If the interviewer (5. ask)
_____ me about my job experience, I (6. tell) _____ the truth. My
brother (7. take) _____ me out when the interview (8. be) _____
over. What will I do if the interviewer (9. not/like) _____ me?

D With a partner, create a perfect future for Alice. Write six sentences with time and *if* clauses. Use one or more of the phrases below in your sentences.

have a baby	buy a new car
find a new job	take a vacation
go to college	get married
meet the man of her dreams	become rich
study English	write a book
climb Mt. Everest	get a job

EXAMPLE: *If Alice gets a job, she'll buy a new car.*

1. _____

2. _____

3. _____

4. _____

5. _____

6. _____

Present and Present Continuous Tenses to Show Future Meaning

Use the present tense to show future meaning when you are talking about schedules or timetables.

The plane **leaves** at 7:00 tomorrow morning.

Only some verbs can be used in the present tense to show future meaning.

These verbs are the most common:

begin	start	arrive	take off	open
end	finish	leave	land	close

Confirmation # EGM562
George and Jean Parker

Flight 206
Depature:
  Washington D.C.   7:00 a.m.
Arrival:
  Chicago   8:04 a.m.

Use the present continuous tense to talk about plans for the future.

Q: What **are** you **doing** this afternoon?

A: I'm **having** a party for my son.

Q: Is he **getting** married tomorrow?

A: No, he's **graduating**.

A Read the sentences below. Circle the verbs in the present continuous tense. Underline the verbs in the present tense. Then listen to the conversation and choose **T** for **True** or **F** for **False**.

1.	Steve is getting married this afternoon.	T	**F**
2.	The ceremony begins at 1:00 p.m.	T	F
3.	Steve isn't going to college right away.	T	F
4.	Mrs. Cho is having a party for Steve.	T	F
5.	Mr. Parker and his wife are coming to the party.	T	F
6.	The store closes at 5:00 p.m.	T	F
7.	Mr. Parker isn't coming by tomorrow.	T	F
8.	The Parkers' flight leaves tomorrow night.	T	F

B Write questions in the present continuous or present tense using the words provided and a helping verb. Then listen again to the conversation from Exercise A and write the answers.

1. When/Steve/graduate

   Question: _When is Steve graduating?_

   Answer: _____

2. What time/graduation/begin

   Question: _____

   Answer: _____

3. Steve/go/to college/right away (**yes-no** question)

   Question: _____

   Answer: _____

4. Mr. Parker and his wife/come to the party (**yes-no** question)

   Question: _____

   Answer: _____

5. What time/store/close

   Question: _____

   Answer: _____

6. What time/the Parkers' flight/leave

   Question: _____

   Answer: _____

7. How/they/get to the airport

   Question: _____

   Answer: _____

> See inside back cover for -ing spelling rules.

C Look at Mr. and Mrs. Parker's plans for their visit to Chicago. Imagine that today is Friday, June 16th. Write six sentences in the present continuous and present tenses to talk about what they are going to do.

June 17th	June 18th
flight leaves: 7:00 a.m.	sleep late
flight arrives: 8:00 a.m.	beach (if it's hot)
rent a car: 8:30	visit more relatives in the evening
get to cousin's house: 9:30	**June 19th**
lunch at Ed's house:12:30	flight leaves: 10:50 a.m.
afternoon: relax, go for a walk	flight arrives: 1:40 p.m.
	get home: 3:00

EXAMPLE: _They arrive in Chicago at 8:00 a.m. tomorrow._

Review

Future Tense, Present and Present Continuous Tenses with Future Meaning, Time and *If* Clauses

A **Dictation** Claire and Art are moving tomorrow. Listen and write what you hear. Then underline the present tense verbs in the *if* and time clauses. Circle the future tense verbs in the main clauses.
Key words: *Seattle, separately, lunchtime, unload, exhausted*

Art and I _____

_____

_____

_____

_____

_____

_____

_____

_____

_____

B Art has a different plan for tomorrow. Complete the sentences below with a verb from the box. You can use some of the verbs more than once. More than one answer is possible.

have	take	get	be	read	want	leave	eat

Claire and I are moving to Seattle tomorrow. She's worried, but I'm not. If we (1.) __get__ there at midnight, that (2.) _____ OK with me. Before we (3.) _____ , I (4.) _____ a big breakfast and (5.) _____ the newspaper. After I (6.) _____ breakfast, I (7.) _____ gas for the truck. During the trip, if I (8.) _____ hungry or tired, I (9.) _____ a break. When we (10.) _____ to our new house, Claire (11.) _____ me to unload the truck right away. But I have another idea. I think I'll take a nap first.

C Complete the chart with information about yourself. Use these sentence patterns.

Routine: *Before I (present tense) . . . , I (present tense) . . .*
Future: *Before I (present tense) . . . (today / tomorrow / tonight), I (future tense) . . .*

	Routine	**Future**
before/go to school	Before I go to school,	
when/be in class		
after/get home		

Look at your partner's sentences. Write six sentences about your partner on a separate piece of paper.

D Complete the chart.

PLANS THAT ARE CERTAIN **(not) be going to**	**PLANS THAT ARE NOT CERTAIN** **(subject + 'll + probably) OR** **(subject + probably + won't)**
I'm not going to go out today.	I probably won't go out today.
I'm going to stay home and relax.	
	They'll probably go to the movies.
We aren't going to be home tomorrow.	
	He'll probably cook dinner.

E Write responses in column B to the statements in column A using **will** or **won't**. More than one answer is possible.

A	**B**
1. I just missed the bus!	I'll drive you.
2. You need to tell me the truth.	
3. Don't forget to call me!	
4. I don't understand this exercise.	
5. I know I don't have a license, Dad. But please give let me drive.	
6. They just left for vacation.	
7. I'm worried about the next test.	

Have Fun

A Communication Gap Work with a partner and talk about Suzanne and Larry's plans for April. One student will be Student A and the other will be Student B.

STEP 1   **Student A:** Go to page 208.
   Student B: Write questions at the bottom of this page. Don't write short answers now.

APRIL

Sunday	Monday	Tuesday	Wednesday	Thursday	Friday	Saturday
2 Today 2:00 visit Alex 7 pm theater	3	4	5	6	7	8
9	10 Suzanne starts Spanish class	11	12	13	14	15 Suzanne's birthday!! Party at Nancy's
16	17 Anniversary	18	19	20	21 go away for the weekend?	22

STEP 2   **Student B:** Ask Student A these questions. Write short answers.

Questions   **Short Answers**

1. What/on/are/going to/they/their anniversary/do

   What are they going to do on their
   anniversary?   ....

2. What/April 16th/on/Larry/do/going to/is

   ....
   ....

3. What time/leave/flight/does/his

   ....

4. What time/Portland/get to/he/does

   ....
   ....

5. What/April 14th/do/going to/they/are/on

   ....

STEP 3   **Student B:** Student A will ask you questions about Suzanne and Larry's plans. Answer the questions with information from the calendar. Use **will probably** to talk about uncertain plans. A question mark (?) on the calendar means the plans are not certain. (Talk, don't write.)

B **Superstitions** Work with a group or your class and make a list of superstitions. Follow this pattern: If 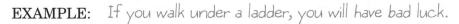 , _____ will _____.

EXAMPLE: If you walk under a ladder, you will have bad luck.

 C **Chant**

Big Plans

Is your son going to finish college this year?
   He's graduating in May.
What's he going to do?
   If he finds a job, he'll move to L.A.
Where's he going to stay in L.A.?
Will he live with his cousin Bob?

   He'll probably get a place of his own
   After he starts his job.
   He's planning to make a movie,
   But he'll need a lot of luck.
   He'll probably work as a waiter,
   Or maybe he'll drive a truck.

Yes-No Questions in the Past, Present, and Future Tenses

To make a **Yes-No** question with **BE**, put the form of **BE** before the subject.

Subject	BE		BE	Subject	
Her parents	are	from Sweden.	Are	her	parents from Sweden?
They	were	here.	Were	they	here?
Her sister	is	going to stay here.	Is	her sister	going to stay here?

To make a **Yes-No** question in the present and past tenses with verbs other than **BE**, use **do, does,** or **did** + the base form of the verb. The base form is the main verb.

Subject	Verb		Helping Verb	Subject	Main Verb	
She	misses	her country.	Does	she	miss	her country?
They	live	in Sweden.	Do	they	live	in Sweden?
She	came	here by herself.	Did	she	come	here by herself?

To make a **Yes-No** question in the future, use **Will** + the base form of the verb.

She **will go** home next month.   **Will** she **go** home next month?

 A Anya is a foreign exchange student from Sweden. She's attending an American high school. Three students are interviewing her. Complete the interview by writing **Are, Were, Did, Do, Does,** or **Will** on each line. Then listen to check your answers.

Marta: _Did_ .... you come to this country by yourself?

Anya: No, I came here with some other students.

Miles: .... you born in a small town?

Anya: No, I wasn't. I was born in a big city.

Tom: .... you having a good time at this school?

Anya: Yes, I'm having a wonderful time.

Marta: .... you think American boys are cute?

Anya: Of course I do!

Miles: .... you ready to go back to your country?

Anya: Not at all!

Tom: .... your family miss you?

Anya: Of course! I miss my family, too!

Marta: .... you leaving soon?

Anya: Uh-huh. I'm leaving in about four weeks.

Miles: .... you come back to visit us?

Anya: I hope so!

B Kim missed the interview with Anya. She's asking Marta about it. Write a **yes-no** question to go with each of Marta's answers.

1. Kim: _Did you interview Anya today?_

   Marta: Yes, I did interview Anya. She was very interesting.

2. Kim: _____

   Marta: Yes, she's leaving the United States in four weeks.

3. Kim: _____

   Marta: Yes, she loves American food, especially hot dogs.

4. Kim: _____

   Marta: Yes, she talked about her family.

5. Kim: _____

   Marta: Yes, she has two brothers and two sisters.

6. Kim: _____

   Marta: No, her parents live in a small town.

7. Kim: _____

   Marta: No, her parents aren't coming to the United States.

8. Kim: _____

   Marta: No, she isn't ready to go back to her country.

9. Kim: _____

   Marta: Yes, the school is going to have a big party for her next week.

10. Kim: _____

    Marta: I don't know. I hope she'll come back and visit us some day.

C Interview a classmate that you don't know well. Write eight **yes-no** questions using some of the words from the box. Then write a paragraph about your classmate on a separate piece of paper.

married	single	absent last week	speak English
born in this country	homesick	look for a job	a grandmother
have children	go to school	miss your country	go home
come to class next week	have a job	go to the movies	stay here

1. _Were you born in this country_____?
2. _____?
3. _____?
4. _____?
5. _____?
6. _____?
7. _____?
8. _____?

Wh Question Review

In **Wh** questions, **What, Where, When, Why, Who,** and **How** come before **BE** or a helping verb.

Wh Questions with BE				**Wh Questions with Other Helping Verbs**		
BE (main verb)				**Helping Verb**		
Where	is	he from?		Where	do	they play cards?
Why	is	she excited?		Why	does	he live there?
How	was	his trip?		When	did	they get there?
BE (Helping Verb)				Who	did	he come with?
Who	are	they living with?		What	will	she do?
What	is	she going to do?		How	will	they get there?

Language Notes:

• Don't put the subject right after the **Wh** word.

Correct: Where was he born?   **Incorrect:** ~~Where he was born?~~

• Don't omit the helping verb.

Correct: Who is she visiting?   **Incorrect:** ~~Who she visiting?~~

A Complete the questions about Pam and her grandfather. Write a **Wh** word and a verb (**BE** or a helping verb) on each line. Then listen to Pam and circle *a* or *b* for each question.

1. _Where was_ he born?
   a. In Asia.   b. In Europe.

2. _____ he come to the United States?
   a. When he was a child.   b. When he was 25.

3. _____ his family get to this country?
   a. By boat.   b. By plane.

4. _____ the trip?
   a. Wonderful.   b. Terrible.

5. _____ he live now?
   a. In New York.   b. In Florida.

6. _____ his friends do at the clubhouse?
   a. Play cards.   b. Eat lunch.

7. _____ Pam be in Florida?
   a. Next week.   b. Next year.

8. _____ she going to Florida?
   a. Her boss is sending her.   b. For a vacation.

B Read Karen's story about coming to the United States. Then write
Wh questions.

When I came to the United States to learn English two years ago, I was very lonely. I was the only person in my class from Taiwan. Then one day I had a strange, but lucky, accident. I fell down on the sidewalk and broke my leg, and a very kind man called an ambulance. He visited me in the hospital, and we talked a lot about our lives. We stayed in touch after I left the hospital, and he taught me English. As we got to know each other, we fell in love. We got married last year. My English is now excellent. And next year we're going to have a baby!

1. Q: *When did Karen come to the U.S.?* ....
   A: Two years ago.

2. Q: ....
   A: Because she was the only person in her class from Taiwan.

3. Q: ....
   A: On the sidewalk.

4. Q: ....
   A: Her leg.

5. Q: ....
   A: A very kind man.

6. Q: ....
   A: Excellent.

7. Q: ....
   A: Next year.

C Look at this timeline of Karen's life.

1980	1990	2002	Now	Future
born in Taiwan	won dance contest	came to the U.S. broke my leg	living in the U.S. married	baby next year graduate school? move to a new house?

Make a timeline of your life. Include past, present, and future years.
Write ten important events on your timeline.

Exchange timelines with a partner. On a separate piece of paper, write five
Wh questions to ask about your partner's life.

Contrast: *Do* as Main Verb and *Do* as Helping Verb

Do, does, and **did** can be helping verbs or main verbs.

Do as a Helping Verb		*Do* as a Main Verb
Negatives	**Questions**	I always do my best.
I don't study.	Do you study?	She does the shopping.
He doesn't study. (When) { Does he study?		We did our laundry.
They didn't study.	Did they study?	I'm doing fine.

Negatives: | She doesn't do anything around the house.

***Do* as a Helping Verb with *Do* as a Main Verb**

Negatives: She doesn't do anything around the house.
He didn't do a good job.

Questions: Do you do your best at school?
When did you do your chores?

Common phrases with *do*: do the laundry, do the shopping, do the dishes, do your work, do something, do nothing, not do anything, do a good job, do homework, do your best, do someone a favor, do chores

A John is talking on the phone with his mother about his roommate. Complete their conversation by filling in each line with a form of **do**. Then listen to check your answers.

Mom: How are you doing?

John: I'm (1.) _____doing_____ fine.

Mom: How's your roommate Paul?

John: He's OK, but he's not a very neat person. He (2.) (not) _____ anything around the house.

Mom: What do you mean?

John: Well, he likes to cook, but after he eats, he never (3.) _____ the dishes. And he never (4.) _____ his laundry. His dirty clothes are in a big pile next to his bed.

Mom: Oh, my! (5.) _____ you tell him to clean up?

John: Yes, I asked him to wash the dishes last night, but he (6.) (not) _____ them. He just left the dishes in the sink.

Mom: That's terrible. (7.) _____ you wash your dishes, John?

John: Of course, Mom. I always clean up!

Mom: Well, tell Paul that he has to do something around the house. Tell him if he (8.) (not) _____ any chores, you'll look for a new roommate. By the way, how's school? (9.) _____ you have a lot of homework?

John: Yes. In fact, I'm (10.) _____ my homework right now.

B Write the answers from Exercise A on the lines. Check **HV** if the answer is a helping verb, **MV** if it is a main verb, or both if the answer includes both.

		HV	MV			HV	MV
1.	doing		✓	6.			
2.	doesn't do	✓	✓	7.			
3.				8.			
4.				9.			
5.				10.			

C Write sentences about John and his roommate to complete the chart.

	Affirmative	Negative	Yes-No Question
Singular/ Present	John does his home-work every day.	John _____ _____.	_____ _____?
Plural/ Present	They _____ _____.	They don't do their homework every day.	_____ _____?
Singular/ Past	He _____ _____.	He _____ _____.	Did he do his home-work yesterday?
Plural/ Past	They did their home-work yesterday.	They _____ _____.	_____ _____?

D Chant

The Poet

Do you know the poet Thomas Jones?
  Of course I do.
  I love his poems.
I do too.
  Does he publish a lot?
No, he doesn't.
He didn't publish a thing last year.
Poets don't make money.
  But how does he live?
  How does he pay the rent?
He teaches.
  What does he teach?
Poetry.

> Remember the possessive adjectives: "his" and "their."

Review

Yes-No and *Wh* Questions Across Tenses, *Do*

A **Dictation** A reporter is interviewing a candidate for governor. Write what you hear. Key words: *improve, successful, whole*

Reporter: Ms. Bates, _what are your_ _____ ?

Ms. Bates: _____

_____

Reporter: _____
when you were a mayor?

Ms. Bates: _____ . I started programs
for parents. _____

Reporter: _____ ?

Ms. Bates: _____ !

Reporter: _____ ?

Ms. Bates: Yes, in some ways. _____
when I'm governor.

Reporter: _____ ?

Ms. Bates: Don't worry. I'll find it.

Reporter: _____ when
you were a mayor?

Ms. Bates: I sure was! _____ ?

_____ !

B Complete the chart with **Wh** questions.

Past Tense	Present Tense	Present Continuous Tense	Future Tense (will or be going to)
Where was the party?	Where	------------------------	Where
	When does the movie start?	------------------------	When
	Why	Why are they doing the shopping?	Why

C **Walk & Talk** Write two **Wh** and two **yes-no** questions with **Do** in the left column. Ask two classmates the questions. Take short notes in the chart. On a separate piece of paper, write eight sentences about your classmates.

EXAMPLE: Q: *Do you do the shopping in your family?*
           A: *No, I don't do the shopping.*

Questions with DO	Student 1	Student 2
1. where/you usually/your homework *Where do you usually do your* *homework* ?		
2. what time/you/homework last night ?		
3. you/the laundry in your house ?	Yes No Sometimes	Yes No Sometimes
4. you/a good job on our last test ?	Yes No So-so	Yes No So-so

D Find the mistakes. Make the corrections.

1. They ~~will~~ *are* going to do the laundry later.
2. You born in this country?
3. Where you were born?
4. Who you visiting?
5. Why you did your homework in the kitchen?
6. Where are you live?
7. When he came home?
8. She don't do her best.
9. Did you did your homework on time?
10. I will doing my laundry in a few minutes.
11. You will leave tomorrow?
12. Where are they come from?
13. Can you make me a favor?
14. Yesterday I relaxed and do nothing.
15. I am do a good job on this exercise.
16. We are doing our best today?

Have Fun

A **Walk & Talk** Write **What** questions on the lines below. Walk around the room and get answers to the questions from three of your classmates. Take short notes in the chart. Then write six sentences about one of your classmates.

1. last night   *What did you do last night?*
2. last weekend
3. after class today
4. tomorrow night
5. every morning
6. every weekend

When?	Student 1 Name:	Student 2 Name:	Student 3 Name:
last night			
last weekend			
after class today			
tomorrow night			
every morning			
every weekend			

Six sentences about (name)

EXAMPLE: *Susana went to the movies last night. She studied English last weekend. She will go home after class today . . .*

B **Communication Gap** Work with a partner. One student will be
Student A, and the other will be Student B.

STEP 1   **Student A:** Go to page 209.
          Student B: Stay on this page. Student A will ask you **yes-no**
          and **Wh** questions about George and Paul's cleaning schedule.
          Answer the questions using information from this calendar.

	Monday	Tuesday	Wednesday	Thursday	Friday	Saturday	Sunday
George	shopping	....	dishes	vacuum the floor	dishes	laundry	....
Paul	....	beds	....	....	....	....	nothing

STEP 2   **Student B:** Ask Student A **yes-no** and **Wh** questions about
          George and Paul's cleaning schedule. Use the information to
          complete the calendar.

EXAMPLE QUESTIONS: *Does Paul do the dishes on Mondays?*
                      What does Paul do on Mondays?

C Chant

Happy Days at Old Mt. Etna

Are you a college student?
    Yes, I am.
Where are you studying?
    I'm at Mt. Etna College.
Is that a school for women only?
    Yes, it is, unfortunately.
Do you like it?
    I don't like it at all.
    I miss the guys.
Why did you choose Mt. Etna?

I didn't choose it.
    My mother did.
Are you going to stay there?
    Yes, I am.
    I'm afraid I'll be there for two
    more years.
Do your parents ever visit you?
    Yes, they do. They love Mt. Etna
    Grandma does too.

LESSON 21

Questions with *Who*

Who questions with BE

Subject	Verb	
Who	is getting	married?
Who	was	at the party?
Who	will be	there?
Who	is going	to make a call?

Who questions with other verbs

Subject	Verb	
Who	has	my phone?
Who	drove	you home?
Who	will drive	there?

When **who** is the subject of a sentence, don't use the helping verbs **do, does,** or **did.**

Correct: Who came to the party?   **Incorrect:** ~~Who did come to the party~~?

When **who** is not the subject of a sentence, use the helping verbs **do, does,** or **did.**

WHO is the subject

	Subject	Verb	
Q:	Who	lives	with Nina?
A:	Dan	does.	

WHO is not the subject

		Helping Verb	Subject	Main Verb	
Q:	Who	does	Nina	live	with?
A:			She	lives	with Dan.

Language Notes:

• Use the **he/she/it** form of the verb when **who** is the subject of a sentence in the present tense.

   Correct: Who wants to get married?   **Incorrect:** ~~Who want to get married?~~

• The contraction for *Who is = Who's.*

• When you want to know about other people, ask, "Who else?"

   Who else is there?

A Nina is talking to her brother, Dan. Read the questions. Write **S** over the subject and **V** over the verb in each question. Then listen to the conversation. Match each question with the correct answer.

_C_ **1.** Who went to a party?   a. A guy she works with.

.... **2.** Who did Nina go to the party with?   b. Jan is.

.... **3.** Who drove her home?   c. Nina did.

.... **4.** Who's getting married?   d. Her brother.

.... **5.** Who is she going to marry?   e. A nice guy.

.... **6.** Who will be very happy?   f. Cindy.

.... **7.** Who did Nina meet at the party?   g. Jan will.

.... **8.** Who has Nina's cell phone?   h. Lots of kids from school.

B Look at these sentences. In each one, change the word **somebody** to **who** and make the statement a question. Put *S* over the subject and *V* over the verb.

1. Somebody is going to marry Jan.

    S   *V*
Who is going to marry Jan?

2. Jan is going to marry somebody.

    V *S* *V*
Who is Jan going to marry?

3. Somebody will be happy.

4. Nina went to the party with somebody.

5. Somebody drove Nina home.

6. Nina met somebody at the party.

7. Somebody is in love with Jan.

8. Jan is in love with somebody.

9. Nina talks to somebody about her life.

C Change these **yes-no** questions to **Who** questions. Then get into a group of at least four students and take turns asking your classmates the **Who** questions. Write eight sentences about your classmates.

EXAMPLES: Student A: *Who's a busy student?*   Student B: *I am!*
                     Student B: *Who has children?*   Students A and C: *I do!*

Yes-No Questions	Who + Verb Questions
1. Are you a busy student?	Who is a busy student?
2. Do you have children?	
3. Were you home last night?	
4. Did you go to a party last night?	
5. Are you tired today?	
6. Are you learning a lot of English?	
7. Do you want to go home after class?	
8. Do you like to dance?	

ANSWERS

EXAMPLE: Elena and Carlos are busy students. / Nobody is a busy student.

1.
2.
3.
4.
5.
6.
7.
8.

LESSON 22

Questions with *How, How far, How often, how long does it take*

There are many kinds of questions with **how**.

		Questions		Answers
	BE or Helping Verb	Subject		
How	do	you	get to work?	I drive./I take the bus.
How far	does	she	live from here?	Five miles.
How often	is	she	late?	Never.*
How long	does	it	take (you) to get there?	Ten minutes.
How	are	your classes?		Great!

*Use frequency words to answer questions beginning with **How often**.

How often do you check your email?

every hour/day/week/month	every two weeks	three times a year
once a day/week/month	twice a day, week, month	every other day

Language Note:

Put **BE** or a helping verb after **how far, how often,** and **how long**.

Correct: How often is your class? **Incorrect:** ~~How often your class is?~~

Correct: How far do you live from here? **Incorrect:** ~~How far you live from here?~~

A Complete the questions with **How** + a helping verb or a form of **BE**. Then listen and circle the correct answer, *a* or *b*.

Conversation 1

1. ....How does.......... Julie get to school?
   a. She takes the bus. b. She drives.

2. .... she live from here?
   a. She lives a few blocks from here. b. She lives far away from school.

3. .... it take her to get here by car?
   a. It depends on the traffic. b. Only a few minutes.

4. .... she go to school?
   a. Every day. b. Three times a week.

Conversation 2

1. .... the museum from here?
   a. About two miles from here. b. About ten miles from here.

2. .... the bus come?
   a. It comes once a day. b. It comes every five minutes.

3. .... it take to get there by bus?
   a. It takes about an hour. b. It takes about ten minutes.

B Kyung is an international student. She is meeting her conversation partner Ted for the first time. Write questions with **How** to go with Kyung's answers.

Ted: Where are you from, Kyung?

Kyung: I'm from Pusan. It's a city in Korea.

Ted: I've never heard of Pusan. (1.) _How far is Pusan from Seoul?_

Kyung: About 500 miles. It's a beautiful city.

Ted: I'd like to go there some day. (2.) _____

Kyung: Oh, I usually go back to Korea once a year. It's such a long trip!

Ted: (3.) _____

Kyung: It takes about fifteen hours by plane.

Ted: That *is* a very long trip. So tell me, do you live in a dorm?

Kyung: No, I live with my relatives in Mason.

Ted: Mason? I don't know where that is. (4.) _____

Kyung: I think it's about 50 miles from here.

Ted: (5.) _____

Kyung: My uncle gives me a ride. He works here.

Ted: That's lucky. So, (6.) _____

Kyung: My classes are wonderful. I'm learning a lot.

C On a separate piece of paper, make questions from these groups of words and phrases. Then ask two students the questions and write eight sentences about their responses.

   1. How often/come to school   **3.** How far/this school/from your house

   2. How/get to school   **4.** How long/usually/take/get to school

D Chant

Questions and Answers

How long does it take to learn to drive?
How long does it take to learn to scuba dive?
How often do you call your brother Bill?
How far do you live from your old friend Jill?
       It doesn't take long to learn to drive.
       It takes a week to learn to scuba dive.
       I call my brother every day at nine.
       Jill's apartment is across the street from mine.

Negative Yes-No and *Why* Questions

Use a negative contraction (**Doesn't, Don't, Isn't, Aren't**) to make negative **Yes-No** and **Why** questions.

Doesn't she have to get up?   Why **don't** we do something fun?

Isn't it time to get up?   **Aren't** they going to school?

Use negative **Yes-No** questions to show surprise or to show that you're not sure about something.

A: I'm going to the movies.   A: I'm going to the movies.

B: **Don't** you have homework?   B: But **aren't** you tired? You didn't sleep last night!

The answer to affirmative and negative **Yes-No** questions is the same.

Question	Meaning	Answer
Do you have homework?	(The speaker is asking for information.)	Yes, I do.
Don't you have homework?	(The speaker is surprised or isn't sure.)	Yes, I do.

Use **Why** in negative questions to ask for reasons.

A: **Why don't** you want to go?   A: **Why aren't** you going to school today?

B: Because I want to go back to sleep.   B: Because my teachers have a meeting.

Use **Why don't you/Why don't we** to give suggestions.

You have free time today. **Why don't you** do your homework?

Language Note:

Don't put the subject right after **Why**. Put the verb after **Why**.

Correct: Why aren't you going to school?   **Incorrect:** ~~Why you aren't going to school?~~

A Read the conversation between Laura and her father, Nick. Write **aren't, doesn't, don't** or **didn't** on each line. Then listen to check your answers.

Nick: Laura! It's time to go to school. (1.) _____Aren't_____ you getting up? (2.) _____ school start at 8:30?

Laura: I don't have to get up early. I'm not going to school today.

Nick: Why (3.) _____ you going?

Laura: (4.) _____ I tell you? We don't have school today.

Nick: Oh right, I forgot! So, what are you going to do?

Laura: I'm going to the movies with my friend Sam.

Nick: But (5.) _____ you have homework to do?

Laura: Yes, we both have homework, but we can do it when we get home.

Nick: Why (6.) _____ you stay home and do your homework together?

Laura: Don't worry, Dad. We don't have much. We can do it tonight.

B Read what Laura and Nick say the next day. Change the statements into negative **yes-no** and **Why** questions.

1. Nick: You went to bed late last night. I'm surprised that you're not tired.

   Q: *Aren't you tired?*

2. Nick: You're not eating any breakfast. I'm surprised that you're not hungry.

   Q: ....

3. Nick: I think you went to the movies, but I'm not sure.

   Q: ....

4. Nick: I don't know why you didn't call me.

   Q: ....

5. Laura: I called you from the theater, but no one was home. I was surprised that you weren't home.

   Q: ....

6. Laura: I suggest that we go out for dinner.

   Q: ....

7. Nick: I suggest that you stay home and do your homework.

   Q: ....

C Answer each of these negative questions with a true short answer. Then make up a question for number 8. Ask a partner the questions.

EXAMPLE: *Aren't you from Taiwan?*   *Yes, I am. OR No, I'm not.*

1. Aren't you from Taiwan?   ....

2. Weren't you in class yesterday?   ....

3. Didn't you do your homework?   ....

4. Isn't your teacher here today?   ....

5. Doesn't your class meet on Friday?   ....

6. Aren't you going to go home soon?   ....

7. Isn't this exercise easy?   ....

8. ....

Negatives Across Tenses

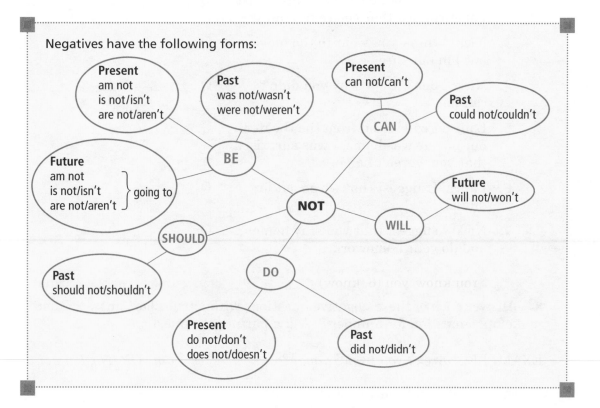

Negatives have the following forms:

Present
am not
is not/isn't
are not/aren't

Past
was not/wasn't
were not/weren't

Present
can not/can't

Past
could not/couldn't

BE

CAN

Future
am not
is not/isn't   } going to
are not/aren't

NOT

Future
will not/won't

SHOULD

WILL

Past
should not/shouldn't

DO

Present
do not/don't
does not/doesn't

Past
did not/didn't

A Read this information about the Olympics. Complete the sentences with the words below. Use **didn't** three times. Then listen to check your answers.

aren't	didn't	doesn't	don't	shouldn't	wasn't	weren't	won't

1. The Olympic games began in Greece more than 2,000 years ago, but the modern Olympics .... begin until 1898.

2. Many countries .... send athletes to the first modern Olympics.

3. There .... many sports at the first modern Olympics, but today, there are hundreds of sports.

4. Not every sport is played in the Olympics. For example, windsurfing is an Olympic sport, but skateboarding and golf ....

5. A long time ago, women .... participate in the Olympics.

6. Some countries still .... send women athletes to the Olympics.

7. Now soccer is popular in the U.S., but it .... popular 30 years ago.

8. The U.S. has many good Olympic teams, but it .... always have the best teams.

9. The 2012 Olympics .... be in New York. They might be in Paris.

10. Some people think that Olympic medal winners .... be able to make a lot of money in advertisements.

windsurfing

skateboarding

medal winner

B Karina doesn't know a lot about sports. She is talking to Jean. Complete their conversation with the correct negative form of the verb in parentheses.

Karina: I think baseball will be the number one sport in France.

Jean: I disagree. Baseball (1. be) _won't be_ the number one sport. Soccer will be the most popular sport there for years to come.

Karina: I think American football and soccer are the same.

Jean: No, American football and soccer (2. be) .... the same. In fact, they're completely different.

Karina: Can soccer players throw the ball?

Jean: Well, the goalie can throw the ball, but the other soccer players (3. touch) .... the ball with their hands.

Karina: That's interesting. I think Pele is a soccer player from Argentina. Am I right?

Jean: Well, Pele is a soccer player, but he (4. be) .... from Argentina. He's from Brazil.

Karina: I think the United States won the World Cup last year.

Jean: No. The United States (5. win) .... the World Cup last year. You know, you (6. know) .... much about sports, Karina!

Karina: But I'm trying to learn. You (7. laugh) .... at me!

C Change these statements to **yes-no** questions. Walk around and ask classmates the questions. When students say **No**, write their names on the lines. Then on a separate piece of paper, write seven negative sentences about your classmates.

Yes-No Questions	Students Who Answer "No"

1. You were a good athlete when you were a child.

   Were you a good athlete when you were a child? ....

2. You played baseball or soccer when you were a child.

   ....

3. You could swim fast when you were a child.

   ....

4. You love sports.

   ....

5. You are a good athlete.

   ....

6. You are taking an exercise class now.

   ....

7. You think you should watch sports on TV every Saturday.

   ....

Review

Who as Subject, Questions with *How*, Negative Questions and Statements

A Dictation It's a Saturday afternoon. Brad Jr. (junior) is asking his father, Brad Sr. (senior), for the car. Write what you hear. Key words: *lawyers, a flat tire*

Brad Jr.: Dad, can I take the car to Adam's house?

Brad Sr.: ....

Brad Jr.: He's a kid in my class.

Brad Sr.: Oh, right. ....

Brad Jr.: Uh-huh.

Brad Sr.: ....

Brad Jr.: ....

Brad Sr.: ....

Brad Jr.: ....

Brad Sr.: Well, ...

Brad Jr.: About ten minutes, I think.

Brad Sr.: ....

Brad Jr.: ....

Brad Sr.: ....

Brad Jr.: ....

Brad Sr.: ....

Brad Jr.: ....

Brad Sr.: Well, ...

Brad Jr.: Dad, *please* let me drive!

B Find the mistakes. Rewrite the questions about Brad Jr. Questions 1-8 should be **Wh** questions. Questions 9-10 should be **yes-no** questions.

1. Who Brad Jr. wanted to visit?   *Who did Brad Jr. want to visit?*

2. Whose going to be at Adam's house?   ....

3. Who will else be there?   ....

4. Why Brad can't ride his bike?   ....

5. Why he didn't ride his bike?   ....

6. Why he isn't cleaning his room?   ....

7. How long it takes to get to Adam's house? ....

8. How often the two boys visit?   ....

9. Haven't Brad a driver license?   ....

10. Doesn't Brad a good driver?   ....

C Complete the chart with negative statements about Brad Sr. and Brad Jr. Put an **X** in places where a sentence is *not* possible.

Present don't/doesn't or isn't/aren't		Present Continuous	Future with Won't	Can't
1. Brad Sr. doesn't eat fast food.	X	Brad Sr. isn't eating fast food.		
2			Brad Jr. won't drive fast.	
3.				Brad Jr. can't be late.
4.		Brad Jr. isn't riding his bike.		
5.	They aren't home.			
6.			They won't stay out late.	

Have Fun

A **Write Dialogs** Working with a partner, write a conversation for each picture. Use your imagination. Have one character show surprise using a *negative* question. Give suggestions with **Why don't**. Perform your dialogs for the class.

1.

A: *Aren't you cold?*

B: *Not really.*

A: *Why don't you put these on?*

B: *Do I have to, Mom?*

2.

A: ....

B: ....

A: Why don't ....

B: ....

3.

A: ....

B: ....

A: Why don't ....

B: ....

4.

A: ....

B: ....

A: Why don't ....

B: ....

B **Walk & Talk** This is your chance to complain! Write six *true* complaints.

1. I'm not ....
2. I don't ....
3. I can't ....
4. Last .... , I didn't ....
5. Last .... , I couldn't ....
6. I wasn't ....

Walk around the room and have short conversations with different classmates.
Follow this example:

> A: *What's wrong? (What's the matter?)*
> B: *I'm tired. Last night, I couldn't sleep.*
> A: *Why not?*
> B: *I was worried about my test.*
> A: *I'm sorry to hear that.*

AUDIO **C** **Chant**

Not So Easy Lifestyle

Do you do the cooking?
　Yes, I do.
How often do you eat out?
　We don't eat out.
　It's too expensive.
How do you get to work?
　We walk to work.
Do you ever take a taxi?
　No, we don't.

We usually walk or take the bus.
　Taxis are too expensive for us.
How long does it take to walk?
　It depends on the weather.
Do you walk in the rain?
Do you walk in the snow?
　Yes, we do!
Good for you!

LESSON
25

Possessive Adjectives, Possessive Pronouns, Possessive Nouns, *Whose*

Adjectives, pronouns, and nouns can show possession.

Possessive Adjectives	Possessive Pronouns	Possessive Nouns
It's **my** jacket.	It's **mine**.	———
They're **your** shoes.	They're **yours**.	———
It's **his** wallet.	That's **his**.	It's **Dad's**.
It's **her** hat.	It's **hers**.	It's **Molly's**.
It's **our** car.	It's **ours**.	———
It's **their** cat.	It's **theirs**.	That's the **Robinsons'** car.
That's **its** food.	———	It's the **street's** name.

Language Notes:

• Don't confuse possessive adjectives and possessive pronouns.

   Correct: These are **their** gloves.   **Incorrect:** ~~These are theirs gloves.~~

• Use **'s** with singular possessive nouns. Don't use **'s** with possessive pronouns.

   Correct: It's my cousin's jacket.   **Incorrect:** ~~It's my cousin jacket.~~

   Correct: It's yours.   **Incorrect:** ~~It's your's.~~

• Use **'s** with plural possessive nouns that don't end in **s**.

   They're **men's** gloves.   They're the **children's** toys.

• Use **s'** with plural possessive nouns that end in **s**.   It's my **parents'** house.

• Use **whose*** to ask questions about possession.

   Whose book is this?   It's my book.   It's mine.   It's Sam's.

   *Don't confuse **Whose** and **Who's**. They sound the same.   **Who's = Who is**

A Molly and her parents just moved into a new house. They are cleaning up after their housewarming party. Listen and complete the sentences with the words you hear.

Mom: What a mess! Please help us clean up, Mollie.

Mollie: OK, Mom. (1. _Whose_) umbrella is this?

Dad: That's (2. _____). Just put it in the closet.

Mollie: OK. And what about this hat?

Mom: Oh. That's (3. _____) hat. I'll take it to (4. _____) house tomorrow.

Mollie: And how about these gloves?

Dad: I think they're (5. _____) gloves.

Mom: Let me see them. No, they're not (6. _____). They're (7. _____) gloves. In fact, they're (8. _____)!

Dad: Are you sure they're (9. _____)? I've never seen them before.

Mom: I'm positive. I bought them for you last year.

Dad: How did they end up in the living room?

78

B Write your answer choices from Exercise A in the column on the left. Check **Possessive Adjective**, **Possessive Pronoun**, or **Possessive Noun** for each choice. No check is needed for **whose**.

		Possessive Adjective	Possessive Pronoun	Possessive Noun
1.	whose	....	....	....
2.	....	....	....	....
3.	....	....	....	....
4.	....	....	....	....
5.	....	....	....	....
6.	....	....	....	....
7.	....	....	....	....
8.	....	....	....	....
9.	....	....	....	....
10.	....	....	....	....
11.	....	....	....	....

C Sandy is leaving a message for Molly's mother Lynn. Find the mistakes in the underlined words and correct them. If an underlined word is correct, write C over the word.

Hi, Lynn. This is your sister ^(C sister's) friend, Sandy. Thank you for inviting us to you're housewarming party. We enjoyed meeting you and all yours friends. I'm sorry to bother you, but I think you have my jacket, and I have your's! Ours jackets look very similar. Mine is beige, and it looks exactly like yours jacket. I'm so sorry. And I think my husband jacket is also at your house. His' is dark brown. Can you call me? My number is 555-1114. Thanks a lot. Bye.

D Chant

Whose books are these?

Whose books are these?
   They're not mine.
   I think those books are Caroline's.
They're not hers.
Hers are green.
   Maybe they are Josephine's.

Whose sneakers are these?
   I think they're Joe's.
   Or maybe those are Jack's.
   Who knows?
Whose glove is this?
   It belongs to Fay.
   She lost it last week in San Jose.

Objects and Object Pronouns

See Appendix F for a list of all pronouns.

Some sentences have subjects, verbs, and objects.

Object Pronouns = me, you, him, her, it, us, them

An object can come right after a verb. An object receives the action of a verb.

Subject	Verb	Object
The boy	threw	the ball.
The boy	threw	it.

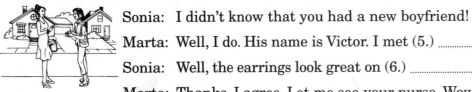

Don't put an adverb between the verb and the object.

Correct: I clean the jewelry carefully.   **Incorrect:** ~~I clean crefully the jewelry.~~

An object usually comes after the preposition.

Subject	Verb	Prep	Object
The earrings	look good	on	Marta.
The earrings	look good	on	her.

Language Note:

Don't omit the object.

Correct: I bought it yesterday.   **Incorrect:** ~~I bought yesterday.~~

A Read the conversation between Sonia and Marta. Fill in each blank with an object pronoun. Then listen to check your answers.

Sonia: Hey, Marta, I love your earrings. Where did you get (1.) __them__?

Marta: My boyfriend bought (2.) _____ for (3.) _____. I wear (4.) _____ every day.

Sonia: I didn't know that you had a new boyfriend!

Marta: Well, I do. His name is Victor. I met (5.) _____ two months ago.

Sonia: Well, the earrings look great on (6.) _____. Victor has good taste.

Marta: Thanks. I agree. Let me see your purse. Wow! Is it new?

Sonia: Uh huh. I bought (7.) _____ on sale at the mall last week. I love (8.) _____.

Marta: It's really beautiful. So, what are you doing these days?

Sonia: Well, my brother and I are taking a grammar class at the college. Grammar isn't easy for (9.) _____.

Marta: Is the class fun?

Sonia: It's difficult, but we're enjoying (10.) _____ very much.

B Look at the underlined word or words in these sentences. Check the correct column for each underlined word or phrase.

	Object after Verb	Object after Preposition	Object Pronoun after Verb	Object Pronoun after Preposition
1. I love <u>your earrings</u>.	✓			
2. He bought them for <u>me</u>.				
3. I found <u>the purse</u> at the mall.				
4. I'm taking classes with <u>my brother</u>.				
5. We're enjoying <u>them</u> very much.				
6. My brother is good at <u>grammar</u>.				
7. He does very well in <u>it</u>.				

C Underline each object in the questions about Marta and Sonia. Then answer the questions in complete sentences. Circle the object pronouns in the sentences you write.

1. Does Marta like Sonia's <u>earrings</u>?

   Yes, she likes ⟨them⟩ very much.

2. How did Sonia get the earrings?

   _____

3. When did Sonia meet Victor?

   _____

4. When did Marta buy the purse?

   _____

5. Where are Sonia and her brother taking their grammar class?

   _____

6. Is grammar easy for Sonia and her brother?

   _____

7. Are they enjoying the grammar class?

   _____

D Ask three classmates the questions in the chart. Take short notes on their responses. Then write three sentences about one of your classmates. Underline the object pronouns.

Name	Do you have something new?	How did you get it/them?	Why do you like it/them?

81

LESSON 27

Reflexive Pronouns

Use reflexive pronouns when the subject and the object of a sentence refer to the same person or thing.

Reflexive pronouns end in **-self** (singular) or **-selves** (plural).

Subject	Verb	Relexive Pronoun	
I	tell	myself	to relax.
You	enjoy	yourself.	
You	made	yourselves	at home.
He	hurt	himself.	
She	should buy	herself	earplugs.
The problem	won't go away	by itself.	
We	never enjoy	ourselves.	
They	don't behave	themselves.	

Use **by** + reflexive pronouns to mean **alone**.

I live by myself. = I live alone.   I did it by myself. = No one helped me.

Common imperative expressions with **yourself** and **yourselves** are:

Help yourself! (Take something.)   Enjoy yourselves! (Have a good time.)

Make yourselves at home! (Feel welcome.)   Take care of yourself!

Behave yourself! (Be good.)   Give yourself a break! (Relax, calm down.)

 A Read Annie's advice column. Circle the reflexive pronouns and underline their subjects. Then listen.

DEAR ANNIE

Dear Annie,
    My sister has three children. They are not bad kids, but they don't behave themselves. They come to our house every Thanksgiving. They run all over the house, and they never say, "please" or "thank you." They help themselves to food wihout asking anyone first. Last year, the oldest

boy fell down and hurt himself because he was running around so much. Each year I tell myself to relax and ignore their bad behavior, but it's hard to do. My husband and I never enjoy ourselves when they visit us.
    Thanksgiving is coming. My husband said, "I want to enjoy myself this year. Let's take a trip on Thanksgiving."
    What should I do? Is my husband right? Should we take a trip? Or should we stay here and invite my sister's family to dinner?

Nervous about Thanksgiving

AUDIO

82

B Read the three responses to the letter from Exercise A. Add reflexive pronouns to each response. Then, tell your classmates which letter you agree with and why.

1. Dear Nervous,

Do you always say, "Make (1.) _yourselves_ at home!" when they come to your house? I bet their house is a mess. So, when they make (2.) _____ at home at your house, they make a mess! I think your husband is right. Give (3.) _____ a break. Take a vacation! Enjoy (4.) _____. Don't invite your sister for Thanksgiving this year.

2. Dear Nervous,

I think your husband is wrong. Invite your sister and her children. They are getting older. Maybe they will behave (1.) _____ this year. Tell your husband to buy (2.) _____ some earplugs. Or maybe your husband should go on vacation by (3.) _____!

3. Dear Nervous,

Tell your sister the truth. Tell her that you and your husband can't enjoy (1.) _____ when her children are running around the house. Your sister needs to tell her children to be more mature. You are their aunt, and you don't want them to hurt (2.) _____ at your house. If you tell the truth, you won't be upset with (3.) _____ anymore. And your sister will thank you for being honest with her.

C Pretend that you are the sister of "Nervous" in Exercise A. It's almost Thanksgiving and your sister hasn't invited you to her house this year. Complete the letter to *Dear Annie* using four of these expressions:

enjoy yourself/myself	do it by myself/himself
behave himself/herself	take care of myself/yourself
cook it by myself/ourselves	ask myself/ourselves

Dear Annie,

My sister usually invites my family for Thanksgiving, but this year she didn't invite us. My husband and I are very upset.

_____

_____

_____

_____

Indefinite Pronouns

> Use indefinite pronouns to talk about people or things without stating who or what they are.
>
> | People | { no one | someone | anyone | everyone |
> |--------|---------|---------|--------|----------|
> | | nobody | somebody | anybody | everybody |
> | Things | nothing | something | anything | everything |
>
> Use the **he/she/it** form of the verb when an indefinite pronoun is the subject of a sentence.
>
> Nobody is here.   Everyone loves parties.
>
> In affirmative sentences, use indefinite pronouns beginning with **some, no, every**, and **any**.
>
> Something is wrong.   No one called me.   Everyone is here.   Anyone can go.
>
> For negative statements and questions, use pronouns beginning with **any** or **every**.
>
> I don't know anything.   He doesn't know everyone.   Did anyone plan a party?
>
> Is anybody home?   Is anything wrong?   Does anyone want a party?
>
> In negative statements, don't use pronouns beginning with **no**.
>
> **Correct:** I don't know anything.   **Incorrect:** I don't know nothing.
>
> Affirmative sentences with **any** mean, "It doesn't matter."
>
> I'll marry anyone.   I'll eat anything.

A Linda and Bob just had dinner to celebrate Bob's birthday. Read the conversation and underline the correct word or phrase. Then listen to check your answers.

Linda: Did you like the restaurant?

Bob: Yes, I did. (1. <u>Everything</u>/Anything) was delicious. But I'm a little disappointed. (2. Everyone/Someone/No one) called me today to say, "Happy Birthday."

Linda: You're right. I'm sorry, Bob. Hey, look! We're passing Uncle Dan's house. Let's stop and say, "Hello."

Bob: I don't think (3. anyone/no one) is home. Hello! Is anyone there? I hear (4. something/anything). I think (5. anyone/someone) is coming.

Uncle Dan: Hi, Bob! Hi, Linda. I'm sorry it took me so long to answer the door.

Bob: Uncle Dan, why is it so dark in here? Is (6. anything/nothing) wrong?

Uncle Dan: No, (7. anything/nothing) is wrong. Come on in.

Bob's friends: Surprise! Happy birthday, Bob!

Bob: Wow! (8. Everyone/No one) is here!

B Write the correct indefinite pronoun on the lines. Sometimes more than one answer is possible. Underline the correct form of the verbs in parentheses.

Linda: Were you surprised about the party?

Bob: I sure was! I didn't see (1.) _anybody_ when I got to the house. (2.) _____ (was/were) very quiet.

Linda: I'm glad you were surprised. Do you want (3.) _____ to drink?

Bob: Thanks, but not right now. I'm going to talk to Uncle Dan. He's standing over there by himself. (4.) _____ (is/are) talking to him. He doesn't know (5.) _____ here.

Bob: Thanks for planning this party, Uncle Dan.

Uncle Dan: It was my pleasure, Bob. I really didn't do (6.) _____. Your friends did all the work. You have wonderful friends. (7.) _____ (love/loves) you very much.

C Complete the questions with **is**, **does**, or **did**. In a group of five or six students, take turns asking and answering the questions. Then write answers to the questions using the words in the box.

everybody/everyone   somebody/someone   nobody/no one   (number) _____ people

1. _Is_ anyone tired?

    Answer: _No, nobody is tired._

2. _____ anybody hungry?

    Answer: _____

3. _____ anyone have a birthday last month?

    Answer: _____

4. _____ anybody going to go home right after this class?

    Answer: _____

5. _____ anyone want to get a snack after this class?

    Answer: _____

6. Write your own question with **anybody** or **anyone**.

    _____

    Answer: _____

Review

Pronouns, Possessive Adjectives, Possessive Nouns

A **Dictation** Diana is complaining to a friend about her mother-in-law. Write what you hear. Key word: *especially*

Nobody understands

_____

_____

_____

_____

_____

_____

_____

B Diana's husband gives his opinion about his mother. Fill in the blanks with **our**, **ours**, **ourselves**, **us**, or **we**.

My mother thinks (1.) _our_ kitchen is her kitchen. But it's
(2.) _____ , not hers! When she comes over, she makes herself at
home. Then she tells (3.) _____ she wants to cook. But we want to
do it (4.) _____! We know she thinks that (5.) _____
can't cook anything. Everyone else likes (6.) _____ cooking.

C Diana's mother-in-law gives her view of the situation. Fill in the blanks with **my**, **mine**, **myself**, **I**, or **me**.

(1.) _____ daughter-in-law doesn't want (2.) _____ to do
anything in her kitchen. She says it's hers, not (3.) _____. She always
wants to take care of everything by herself, so (4.) _____ never enjoy
(5.) _____ when I visit. Sometimes (6.) _____ ask
(7.) _____ why my wonderful son married her!

D Add apostrophes to these sentences where necessary.

1. His mother's house is beautiful.
2. His parents house is beautiful.
3. That womans husband is a great cook.
4. Those womens husbands are great cooks.
5. The childrens toys are all over the house.
6. The childs shoes are under the bed.
7. Dianas friends visited her.
8. That girls mother is late.
9. The babys bottle fell off the table.
10. The babies toys are expensive.

E Complete the charts.

AFFIRMATIVE Verb + *nothing*	NEGATIVE Verb + *not* + *anything*	YES-NO QUESTION with *anything*
He knows nothing about that.	He doesn't know anything about that.	Does he know anything about that?
He knew nothing about that.		
They did nothing about that.		
	You don't know anything about that.	
	I can't do anything about that.	
She'll probably do nothing about that.		Will she do

There + (not) BE + *anyone/anybody*	There + BE + *no one/nobody*	QUESTION with *anyone/anybody*
	There was nobody home.	Was anyone home?
There wasn't anybody there.		
There isn't anyone in the kitchen.		

F Join a team of five to eight students and choose a leader. Secretly give the leader something you own: a photo, a watch, your glasses, etc. The leader will ask who owns the items.

EXAMPLE: *Leader:* *"Whose watch is this?"*
             Student A: *"It's Chang's."*
             Student B: *"No it isn't. It's mine."*

Have Fun

A Crossword Puzzle

Across

1. The dog is having a problem walking. It hurt ....

4. Is .... wrong? You look worried.

6. He's strong. He can carry it .... himself.

7. Can you help ....? We need help!

10. She enjoyed .... at the party.

11. It isn't .... Mine is red.

13. I can learn how to use it. I can teach ....

14. That's our computer. That's ....

15. They don't need help. They can work by ....

Down

2. This isn't our computer. It's Sandy's and Bill's. It's ....

3. The room is empty. I don't see .... there.

5. Welcome to our home! Come in and make .... comfortable!

8. It's .... She bought it.

9. I don't like doing puzzles, but I know that almost everybody else .... them.

12. .... laptop is that? It isn't mine.

B Chant

I Love Your Necklace

I love your necklace.

    Thank you.

Where did you get it?

    I made it myself.

You made it yourself? I've never seen anything like it.

It's wonderful.

    Thank you.

    I'm glad you like it.

Your house is great. It's so quiet. Nobody can bother you.

    I built it myself.

You built it yourself? Really?

    Yes, I'm an architect.

You're so talented.

And I love the paintings. Who did them?

    I did them myself.

You're a painter, too?

    Yes, I am.

I've never met anybody like you. You're amazing!

LESSON 29 Count and Non-Count Nouns

See the rules for -s spelling on the inside of the back cover. See Appendices L and M for more information.

There are two different kinds of nouns: count and non-count.

Count nouns can be singular or plural. You can count them with numbers.
Use **a**, **an**, or **one** before singular count nouns. Use **one** when you want to specify *only* one.
Use **-s** with plural nouns.
Singular: a flashlight, **one** flashlight   **Plural:** **two** flashlights

Non-count nouns have only one form. You can't count them.
Don't use **a**, **an**, or **one** with non-count nouns. Don't add **-s** to non-count nouns.

Correct	Incorrect
I bought **sunscreen**.	~~I bought a sunscreen.~~
I forgot her **homework**.	~~I forgot her homeworks.~~

Use the **he/she/it** form of the verb with most non-count nouns.
    My medicine **is** expensive.   The chocolate **looks** delicious.

Types of non-count nouns:
- Some non-count nouns are made up of very small things that are hard to count.
  hair   fur   sand   salt   rice   sugar
- Some non-count nouns are abstract, not concrete. We can't feel them or touch them.
  advice   help   information   news   traffic   weather
  fun   knowledge   music   pollution   violence   work
- Some non-count nouns are semi-solids and liquids.
  butter   coffee   lotion   soup   toothpaste
  cheese   ice   soap   tea   water
- Some non-count nouns name groups or types of things.
  furniture   food   jewelry   clothing   money
- Some non-count nouns are always plural. Use the **they** form of the verb with these nouns.
  clothes, glasses, pants, jeans, shorts, scissors, groceries.
  His clothes **are** in his backpack.   The sunglasses **are** expensive.

A Listen to Ted, Kay, and Jenny talk about the things they brought and the things they forgot to bring on their camping trip. Put a check (✔) by the things they remembered to bring.

| ...... flashlights | ...... jackets | ...... towel | ...... soap | ...... sleeping bag |
| ...... toothbrushes | ...... toothpaste | ...... homework | ...... book | ...... medicine |

90

B Put the nouns from Exercise A in the correct column. Add two more items needed for camping to each column. Write **a** or **an** before each singular count noun.

Singular Count Nouns	Plural Count Nouns	Non-Count Nouns
a towel		

C Write **SC** (singular count), **PC** (plural count), or **N** (non-count) over each **bolded** noun. Then write **a**, **an**, or **Ø** on each of the blank lines. Circle the correct verb form in the parentheses.

Kay: There's (1.) _____a_____ good general **store** near here. They sell
everything. What do we have to buy?

Ted: Well, we need (2.) _____ **toothpaste** and (3.) _____
flashlight. Jenny's (4.) _____ **homework** (is/are) at home, so
there's nothing we can do about that.

Ted: True. What else do we need? It's so sunny here. I think Jenny needs
(5.) _____ **hat** and (6.) _____ **sunscreen**.

Kay: Good idea. Hey—look over here. Free samples of (7.) _____
chocolate!

Ted: Mmm. It (is/are) delicious.

Kay: And look! They sell (8.) _____ **pillows**. This store is amazing. I'd
love (9.) _____ extra pillow. And I also need (10.) _____
sunglasses.

Ted: But Kay, these sunglasses (is/are) expensive. We need to save (11.)
_____ **money** for our tour of the national park tomorrow.

D In teams of four students, you will have five minutes to make a list of items to take to the beach. Use a separate piece of paper and follow the format below. Circle **S** (singular), **P** (plural), or **N** (non-count) for each noun on your list. The team with the most nouns is the winner.

Noun	What Kind of Noun Is It?
....	S P N

Quantity Words

Use quantity words before plural count nouns and non-count nouns to describe how much or how many of something exists.

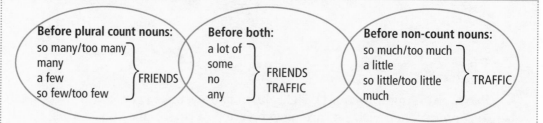

Before plural count nouns:
so many/too many
many
a few
so few/too few } FRIENDS

Before both:
a lot of
some
no
any } FRIENDS
TRAFFIC

Before non-count nouns:
so much/too much
a little
so little/too little
much } TRAFFIC

Use **no** and **some** in affirmative statements. Use **any** in negative statements and questions.

Affirmative
There are **no** museums.
It has **some** museums.

Negative
It doesn't have **any** museums.
Does it have **any** museums?

Use **much** in negative sentences.
The town **doesn't** have **much** pollution.

Use **a lot of** in affirmative and negative sentences.
The town has **a lot of** pollution.

So and Too

Use **so much/too much** with non-count nouns.
I have **so much** time to relax.   *positive meaning*
There is **too much** traffic.   *negative meaning*

*You must use **so** or **too** with **much** in an affirmative sentence.
Correct: There is too much work to do.   **Incorrect:** ~~There is much work to do.~~

Use **so many/too many** with plural count nouns.
There are **so many** nice beaches in Hawaii.   *positive meaning*
There are **too many** people in Honolulu.   *negative meaning*

A Read the sentences and circle the correct quantity word or phrase in the parentheses. Write **C** (count) or **NC** (non-count) over each underlined word. Then listen to Max's phone message and circle **T** for **True** or **F** for **False**.

Laketown

Central City

NC
1. Laketown has (so many/**so much**) beautiful <u>scenery</u>.   (T)   F
2. There aren't (no/any) <u>movie theaters</u> in Laketown.   T   F
3. I'll make (a lot of/much) <u>money</u> in Laketown.   T   F
4. Laketown has (no/any) <u>air pollution</u>.   T   F
5. I don't have (no/any) <u>friends</u> in Central City.   T   F
6. There are only (a little/a few) <u>restaurants</u> in Central City.   T   F
7. There aren't (many/much) cheap <u>apartments</u> in Central City.   T   F
8. There's (only a little/only a few) <u>traffic</u> in Central City.   T   F
9. I don't have (many/much) <u>time</u> to make my decision.   T   F

B Complete the sentences with **so many**, **so much**, **too many**, or **too much**. More than one answer is possible.

1. Central City has _____too much_____ crime. It's a little dangerous at night.

2. I love to go out to eat. There are _____ restaurants there.

3. The streets are crowded. There are _____ cars.

4. The air is terrible. Central City has _____ pollution.

5. Central City is crowded. There are _____ people.

6. I love Central City. I have _____ fun there at night.

7. I love the excitement of Central City. There are _____ things to do.

C Rewrite the sentences. Use **much**, **many**, **no**, or **any**.

1. Central City has a lot of restaurants. ___Central City has many restaurants___.

2. Laketown doesn't have any museums. _____

3. Laketown doesn't have any pollution. _____

4. Laketown has a lot of houses for rent. _____

5. Central City has no pollution. _____

6. People in Central City are busy.
   They don't have a lot of free time. _____

7. Central City has no nice scenery. _____

D Write four sentences about good things in your city or town and four sentences about things that aren't good. Use the quantity words in the chart on page 92. Then tell a classmate about your city or town.

_____
(name of city/town)

Good Things	Things That Aren't Good
EXAMPLE:	
It doesn't have any factories.	It has too much traffic.
1.	1.
2.	2.
3.	3.
4.	4.

31

A/An vs. *The*

Use **a/an** to introduce a noun for the first time
Use **the** to talk about the same noun again.

A cat walked in.
The cat scared some mice.

Use **the** when there is only one of something.

The cat pushed the door open.

Use **the** with these nouns. The idea is that there is only *one*.
• rooms in a house: the kitchen, the bathroom, the living room, the dining room
• parts of a room: the ceiling, the floor, the door, the window, the corner*
• parts of a school: the library, the office, the bookstore, the gymnasium (the gym)
• the world: the sun, the moon, the earth, the sky, the ground
• things that relate to countries: the government, the economy, the army, the navy
• things in the neighborhood: the airport, the train station, the bank, the post office
*You can say **the window** and **the corner** even when there are more than one in a
 room. The idea is that the listener knows which one you're talking about.

Language Notes:
• Always use the with same.
Correct: The mice want the same food.   **Incorrect:**   ~~The mice want same food.~~
• Always use the with superlatives.
The baby mouse was the most scared.
• Don't use the before proper nouns.
Correct: Cinderella went to a ball and met a prince.
Incorrect: ~~The Cinderella went to a ball and met a prince.~~

A Read this story. Write **a** or **the** on the lines. Then listen to check your
answers.

I'm going to tell you (1.) ____a____ famous **joke**. Once upon a time,
(2.) _____ **mother mouse** was running across (3.) _____
floor in the kitchen. (4.) _____ **mother mouse** was with her
three children. Suddenly, (5.) _____ **mother mouse** heard (6.)
_____ **cat**. (7.) _____ **cat** came into (8.) _____
kitchen. (9.) _____ **baby mice** were very scared. Then (10.)
_____ **mother mouse** said, "Bow wow!" and (11.) _____
cat ran away. (12.) _____ **mother mouse** turned to her children
and said, "See! I told you that it is very important to learn (13.)
_____ **foreign language!**"

B Write **a**, **an**, or **the** and the **bolded** nouns from Exercise A in the correct columns.

a—introduce noun	**the**—there is only one	**the**—the noun again
a joke		

C Find the mistakes. Make the corrections.

1. Once there was ~~the~~ poor girl.
2. The poor girl's name was the Cinderella.
3. She lived in old house with her stepmother and two mean sisters.
4. Every day, she cleaned kitchen and cooked.
5. It was hardest job in world.
6. Then she met prince at big party.
7. Prince fell in love with her.
8. Her sisters wanted to marry same man.
9. A prince found Cinderella's house.
10. When she opened door, he said, "Will you marry me?"

D Write a fairy tale or another kind of story from your childhood. Follow the example in Exercise C. Circle all the articles you use. Share your story with your classmates.

Once

Article vs. No Article

LESSON 32

To talk about things in general (to *generalize*), use plural count nouns or non-count nouns with no article. Don't use **a**, **an**, or **the**.

General Statements	Specific Statements
Plural Count Nouns I love **dogs**. = I love dogs in general. ∅ ← → plural noun	I love **the** dog. = I love a specific dog. I love **the** dogs. = I love a specific group of dogs. I have **a** dog. = I have one specific dog.
Non-Count Nouns I love **music**. = I love music in general. ∅ ← → non-count noun	I love **the** music. = I love the music playing now. I love this specific music.

Language Notes:

• To generalize, make count nouns plural.

Correct: He doesn't like computers.

Incorrect: ~~He doesn't like computer.~~

• Use the word **especially** to give an example after a generalization.
He loves music, **especially** jazz.

A The Question Lady from a local newspaper asked four people about what they love and dislike. Look at the underlined nouns. Write **G** over the general nouns. Write **Sp** over the specific nouns. Then listen.

Well, I love (1.) <u>hats</u>. I love big hats, small hats, berets, cowboy hats... all hats. (2.) <u>The hat</u> that I'm wearing is from the 1940s. What do I dislike? Hmm. Well, I don't like (3.) <u>spiders</u>. Spiders really scare me.

I love (4.) <u>music</u>. My favorite music is (5.) <u>jazz</u>. I don't like (6.) <u>opera</u> very much. Opera is very difficult to understand. My aunt took me to (7.) <u>an opera</u> once, and I fell asleep.

I love (8.) <u>candy</u>, especially chocolate. I think that (9.) <u>chocolate</u> is good for you. I also love (10.) <u>jellybeans</u>. Oh, I also love (11.) <u>cute guys</u>, especially my boyfriend. He's (12.) <u>a really cute guy</u>.

B The Question Lady is interviewing a teenage boy. Add -**s** to the general nouns. Add **a** before the specific nouns.

I love (1.) _____computer**s**_____. My mother hates them, but I love them. My father bought me (2.) _____computer_____ last year. It's (3.) _____wonderful computer_____. What do I dislike? Well, I dislike (4.) _____test_____. We have (5.) _____grammar test_____ tomorrow and I'm not happy about it. (6.) _____Test_____ make me nervous.

C In each pair of sentences, only one sentence is a correct general statement. Circle the letter of the correct sentence.

1. a. The snakes scare me.   (b.) Snakes scare me.

2. a. The life is expensive here.   b. Life is expensive here.

3. a. American house cost a lot.   b. American houses cost a lot.

4. a. Children need exercise.   b. Children need the exercise.

5. a. Motorcycle is dangerous.   b. Motorcycles are dangerous.

6. a. I love fruit, especially the peaches.   b. I love fruit, especially peaches.

D Use the words below to make general statements about your native country. Add a frequency adverb (**always**, **usually**, **often**, **sometimes**, **rarely**, **never**) to each sentence. If the U.S. is your native country, write about your parents' native country.

1. Children in _Spain always enjoy holidays and festivals._

2. Women in _____

3. Teenagers in _____

4. Life in _____

5. Men in _____

6. Grammar teachers in _____

7. Food in _____

8. Television programs in _____

9. Houses in _____

10. (Choose your own topic.) _____

Another, The other(s), Another one and *The other one(s)*

Another means *one more*. Another = **an + other**.
We have two children, but we want a big family. We want another child.

The other means *the last one* in a group. It means a specific person, place, or thing.
We have two children. One is a boy, and the other is a girl.

Another, other, and **the other** can be used as adjectives.
They have two girls and one boy. They want to have another boy.
We don't have hats, but we have other baby clothes.
We have four kids. Two are boys, and the other kids are girls.

Another (one) and **the other (one)** can be used as pronouns.
We have two kids, and we want another (one).
We have two kids. One is a boy, and the other (one) is a girl.
We have four kids. Two are boys, and the others (OR: the other ones) are girls.

Language Notes:
- Use **another** with singular count nouns.
- Don't use **another** with plural nouns or with non-count nouns.

| **Correct:** | Do they want another child? | **Incorrect:** | ~~Do they want another children?~~ |
| | I have news. | | ~~I have another news.~~ |

- Don't add **-s** to **other** when **other** is an adjective.

| **Correct:** | They have other daughters. | **Incorrect:** | ~~They have others daughters.~~ |

 A Read the conversation. Circle the correct word or phrase in parentheses. Then listen to check your answers.

Mark: It's a little cold here. Do you have (1. *another*/the other) table?

Waiter: Well, right now there are only two other free tables. One is near the door, and (2. another one/the other one) is over here, by the kitchen. Would you like that one?

Mark: Yes, we would. Thank you.

A few minutes later . . .

Waiter: We have two specials tonight. One is roast beef and (3. another one/the other) is salmon.

Linda: I'll have the roast beef. And, sir, could you please get me (4. another one/another/the other) glass? This one is a little dirty.

Waiter: Oh, I'm sorry. Certainly!

Linda: Mark, I have some important news.

Mark: What is it?

Linda: We're going to have (5. another/the other/the other one) baby!

Mark: Wow! That's great news!

Linda: I wonder if we'll have (6. another/other) son or (7. another/other) daughter. I'm so excited!

B Look at your answers in Exercise A. Put each sentence in the correct column.

Not the last one(s). More are possible.

<u>Do you have another table available?</u>

....

....

....

The last one(s). There are no more.

....

....

C Find the mistakes. Make the corrections.

1. Mark and Linda have two children. One is a boy, and ^the other one is a girl.

2. They have two children, and they want other one.

3. One of their two children is five and another one is three.

4. Their daughter doesn't want other brother.

5. They already have a crib, but they need another furniture for the new baby.

6. They have a stroller, but it's old. They will need to buy the other stroller.

D Chant

Hotel Smash

Let's stay another week!
I love this place.
    Another week? In this awful hotel?
We can always find another hotel. That's easy.
We can move to the other one tonight.
    What other one?
You know the one,
The other one right on the beach.
    Not the one with the all-night disco!
Yes, that's the famous Hotel Smash.
I love their all-night disco.
There's not another place like it in the world.
I love that Hotel Smash.
    Isn't there another small hotel?
    I don't want to hear another disco.
We'll never find another place like the Smash.
And I love that all-night disco.

Review

Count and Non-Count Nouns, Quantity Words; Articles, *Other, Another*

A Dictation Lily is a college student and she is talking to her father about possible careers. Write what you hear. Key words: *biology, reporters*

Lily:	I don't know
Dad:	
Lily:	
Dad:	
Lily:	
Dad:	
Lily:	
Dad:	

B Complete the chart with sentences from Exercise A.

	Quantity Word +	Count Noun
1. I can give you	some	ideas .
2.		do.

	Quantity Word +	Non-Count Noun
3. I want to have to travel.		
4. No, doctors have		.
5. But most reporters don't make		.

	a/an	Singular Count Noun
6. You can be		.
7. You can be		.
8. Or		.

	another/ the other(s)/other(s)
9. I have idea.	
10. One makes $100,000 and makes $95,000.	

General Statements ∅ Plural Noun	Specific Statements *The* Noun
11. No, _____ have too much work.	13. _____ _____ on Channel 4 make $100,000 a year.
12. _____ travel a lot.	

C Find the mistakes. Make corrections.

1. His blue jeans ~~is~~ *are* ten years old!

2. Relax! We have much time.

3. Look! We have same backpack.

4. I love you too much!

5. I love classical musics.

6. I don't like bug.

7. We have many homeworks tonight.

8. There's a few traffics today.

9. The others students are in the library.

10. Can we rent another movies?

11. I have many informations for you.

12. We need to buy furnitures.

13. Can you give me an advice?

14. My another jewelry is at home.

15. There are four review exercises.
    We did three. Now, let's do other exercise.

D Look at the pictures below and write a story. Create two sentences for each picture. Use the past tense and underline **a, an** and **the** in your sentences.

A

B

<u>A woman walked to a bench on campus.</u>

....

....

....

C

D

....

....

....

....

Have Fun

A **"Find Someone Who..." Bingo** Write **Yes-No** questions to ask your classmates. When a student says, "Yes" or "Sometimes," write his or her name in the box. The first person to get five names in a straight line [vertical (|), horizontal (—), or diagonal (/) (\ )] is the winner.

EXAMPLE:
A: *Are you taking another class?*
B: *No, I'm not.*
A: *OK. Thank you.*

A: *Are you taking another class?*
B: *Yes, I am.*
A: *Great! What's your first name?*

is taking another class *Are you taking another class?* name	is taking two classes	eats too much candy	eats too many cookies	usually wears jeans
loves chocolate	wants a piece of chocolate right now	can give (me) some advice	loves apples	wants an apple right now
had a lot of homework last night	has a lot of homework every day	**Free Space**	usually has too much homework	usually has too many assignments to do
likes computers	has a computer	has a car and wants another one	thinks there's too much traffic around here	thinks there are too many SUVs around here
likes music	plays a musical instrument	drinks tea often	is going to the supermarket this weekend	has some free time this weekend

B Chant

Nice Job

She has a lot of friends in Texas,
A few good friends in Maine,
A couple of friends in Paris,
And one old friend in Spain.

She meets a lot of people,
Both men and women, too.
She doesn't make much money,
And she has a lot to do.

She has a new boyfriend in Turkey,
Another one in France.
She met another guy in Greece
Who really loves to dance.

She loves big dogs and horses,
But she's always in the sky.
Her office is a jet-plane,
And she really loves to fly.

As...as, Not as...as

See Lesson 29 and Appendices L and M for more information on nouns.

Use **as...as** with an adjective to show that two nouns are equal or not equal.

An SUV is as big as a minivan.   An SUV isn't as safe as a minivan.

Use **as...as** with an adverb to show that two verbs are equal or not equal.

She drives as fast as he does.   She doesn't drive as fast as he does.

Use **as many...as** and **as much...as** to show that two amounts are equal or not equal.

Use **as many...as** with count nouns.

SUVs can carry as many passengers as minivans.

Use **as much...as** with non-count nouns.

An SUV doesn't have as much space as a minivan.

Use **almost** or **nearly** with **as...as** to show that two things are slighty less than equal.

A minivan is almost/nearly as expensive as an SUV.

A The Garcia Family is shopping for a new family car. Read the conversation and circle the correct word or phrase in the parentheses. Then listen to check your answers.

Juan: I think we should buy an SUV. It (1. is as big / (is as big as)) a minivan, and we can drive it anywhere.

Maria: But an SUV (2. isn't safe as / isn't as safe as) a minivan. SUVs roll over easily. We can get hurt. And a minivan holds more people.

Juan: Some SUVs carry (3. as many / as much) passengers as a minivan. And you know I like to drive fast. A minivan (4. doesn't go as / goes) fast as an SUV.

Maria: I don't care about speed. You know I don't drive (5. as fast as / as slow) you do. We have kids. I want a car that (6. is as safe as / isn't safe as) the one we have now. And we need space for our luggage on trips. An SUV doesn't have (7. as much / as many) space as a minivan. Also, SUVs are more expensive.

Juan: Well, an SUV has almost (8. as much / as many) space as a minivan. But you're right, we should get the minivan. I want you to be happy.

minivan   SUV

B The Garcia family went to Blues Restaurant to celebrate buying their new car. Afterwards, they compared Blues to their favorite restaurant, Rocky's. Look at the chart and complete the sentences below with **as...as**.

Blues Restaurant		Rocky's Restaurant	
Food	bad	Food	good
Waiters	friendly	Waiters	friendly
Servings	small	Servings	large
Tables	clean	Tables	dirty
Prices	low	Prices	high
Service	fast	Service	fast
Music	not loud	Music	loud

1. The food at Blues *isn't as good as the food at Rocky's.*

2. The waiters at Rocky's _____

3. The servings at Blues _____

4. At Rocky's, they don't clean the tables _____ **at Blues.**

5. At Rocky's, they serve the food _____ **at Blues.**

6. The prices at Rocky's _____

7. The music at Blues _____

C Chant

The Thing

It's not as big as a truck.
It's not as noisy as a duck.

It's not as expensive as a trip to Peru.
It's not as tiny as a tent for two.

It's almost as awful as the sound of a flea.
It's almost as tall as a coconut tree.

It's as warm as a beautiful day in June.
It's as bright and shiny as a new full moon.

It's as dangerous as a sailboat without a sail.
It's as sad as a tiger without a tail.

35 *Too and Enough*

Use **too** and **enough** to talk about the amount or quality of something.

Too has a negative meaning. It means *more than what is good*.

	too	adjective/adverb	
Katie's house is	too	small.	
Do people drive	too	fast	through the neighborhood?

Don't confuse **too** and **very**.
Very can have a negative or positive meaning.
Negative: The school is very far away, so we need to drive.
Positive: Katie and Ryan are very happy together.

Enough has a positive meaning. It means *the right amount*.

	adjective/ adverb + enough	enough + noun
Is the neighborhood	safe enough?	They have enough money for a new house.
People drive	slowly enough.	They spend enough time with their kids.
Incorrect: ~~People drive enough slowly.~~		**Incorrect:** ~~They spend time enough.~~

A Katie and Ryan are trying to decide which house to buy. Listen to their conversation. Circle **Positive** when you hear a sentence that has a positive meaning, and circle **Negative** when you hear a sentence that has a negative meaning.

1.	Positive	Negative	**5.**	Positive	Negative
2.	Positive	Negative	**6.**	Positive	Negative
3.	Positive	Negative	**7.**	Positive	Negative
4.	Positive	Negative	**8.**	Positive	Negative

B Katie and Ryan moved into their new house. Unscramble the words in parentheses, and write sentences about life in their new house.

1. (new house is/enough/their/big) _Their new house is big enough._

2. (Ryan/far/live/too/from his job/doesn't) ....
....

3. (aren't/neighbors/too/noisy/their) ....
....

4. (enough/Ryan/gets home/early) ....
....

5. (Ryan/enough/with the kids/now/can spend/time) ....
....

6. (there/enough/is/for their/space/dog) ....
....

C In the column on the left, use the words in parentheses to write questions. Write short answers to your questions in the middle column. Then ask a partner the questions and write their short answers on the right.

Question	You	Your Partner
(neighborhood/safe enough) _Is your neighborhood safe enough?_		
(house or apartment/too small) ?		
(job/close enough to your home) ?		
(house or apartment/too expensive) ?		
(school/close enough to your home) ?		

D On a separate piece of paper, write five sentences about you and your partner using information from the chart in Exercise C. Use **but** in your sentences when you and your partner have different answers to the same question.

EXAMPLE: _Our neighborhoods are safe enough._
My house is big enough, but my partner's apartment is too small.

CVC=Consonant+
Vowel+Consonant

Use a comparative adjective + **than** to compare TWO nouns.
San Francisco is big. Lima, Peru is **bigger**. OR Lima is **bigger than** San Francisco.

For one-syllable adjectives:
- add **-er**.
- add **-r** when the adjective ends in **e**.
- double the final consonant and add **-er** when the adjective ends in **CVC**, but not when the adjective ends in **w**.

Are people are warmer in your hometown?
Stores stay open later in big cities.

Is Lima is bigger than San Francisco?
The buildings in San Francisco are newer.

For two-syllable adjectives that end in y:
drop the **y** and add **-ier**.

People in my hometown are friendlier.

For most adjectives that have two or more syllables and don't end in y:
- use **more**.
- use **less** to say "not as much."

My new house is more expensive.
My old house is less expensive.

Adjectives with irregular comparative forms: **good → better   bad → worse   far → farther**

Who/Which Questions:
To compare two people, ask:

Who is older, your brother or your sister?
Who is friendlier?

To compare two places or things, ask:

Which city is bigger, Lima or New York?
Which is bigger?

Language Note:
Use **much** + a comparative adjective to make a stronger comparison of two things.
The buildings are much older.   Life there is much more/much less expensive.

A Miguel and Tim are talking about San Francisco and Lima. Listen to the conversation and put **L** for Lima or **SF** for San Francisco next to each sentence.

San Francisco

Lima

1. ...... It's more beautiful.

2. ...... The buildings are newer.

3. ...... The people seem less friendly.

4. ...... Public transportation is more convenient.

5. ...... The stores close earlier.

6. ...... The roads are narrower.

7. ...... The traffic is much worse.

8. ...... The food is better.

B Miguel's mother calls him and asks him to compare his new job and apartment to his old job and apartment. Change the bolded word in each group into a comparative adjective, and write a question.

1. new job/**interesting**/old job

Is your new job more interesting than your old job? _____?

2. your English/**good**/now/before

Is _____?

3. **patient**/your new boss or your old boss

Who _____?

4. your new salary/**high**/old salary

Is _____?

5. apartment/**close** to/work

Which _____?

6. the people in your new neighborhood/**friendly**/people in your old neighborhood

Are _____?

7. apartment/**old**/this one or the other one

Which _____?

8. the stores in your new neighborhood/**expensive**/stores in your old neighborhood

Are _____?

C   Part 1: Miguel decided to go back to Lima, and he's looking for an apartment. Look at the pictures of two places for rent. On a separate piece of paper, write six sentences comparing the two apartments. Share your sentences with a partner.

Apartment A

$850/month
Built: 1990

Apartment B

$250/month
Built: 1972

Part 2: Ask your partner to compare one of these pictures to where he or she lives now. First, write three questions with **Which**. Then ask your partner the questions.

EXAMPLE: _Which apartment do you think is newer, this one or yours?_

37 Superlative Adjectives

Use "few"/"fewer"/ "the fewest" with countable nouns. See Lesson 29.

Use **the** + a superlative adjective to compare THREE or more nouns.

For one-syllable adjectives:
- add **-est**.
- add **-st** when the adjective ends in **e**.
- double the final consonant and add **-est** when the adjective ends in **CVC**, but not when the adjective ends in **w**.

Central College is the oldest.
Eric's class is the latest.

His class is the biggest.
Is Josh's car the newest?

For two-syllable adjectives that end in y:
drop the y and add **-iest**.

Is the biology teacher the busiest?

For most adjectives that have two or more syllables and don't end in y:
- use **the most**.
- use **the least**.

That school is the most popular.
It has the least expensive dorms.

Adjectives with irregular superlative forms:

| good → the best | bad → the worst | far → the farthest | less → the least |

One of the + superlative adjective + *plural* noun:

Correct: One of the best restaurants in town is the Pizza Factory.
Incorrect: ~~One of the best restaurant in town is the Pizza Factory.~~
Incorrect: ~~One of best restaurant in town is the Pizza Factory.~~

A Eric is trying to decide which college to attend. Listen and put a check (✓) in the correct box.

	East College	**Central College**	**West College**
the lowest tuition			
one of the best music programs			
the farthest from home			
the least expensive dorms and food			
the highest tuition			
the biggest college			
the most students			
the fewest students			

B Eric is asking for advice from his new roommate at East College. In each blank space, write the correct form of the superlative adjective and noun in parentheses. Be sure to use **the**.

Eric: Where can I meet people? I don't know anyone yet.

Josh: Well, one of (1. easy/place) *the easiest places* .... to meet people is Club 21. There's dancing and everyone is very friendly.

Eric: I need to find a cheap place to eat, too.

Josh: (2. not expensive/restaurant) .... is The Pizza Factory. We all eat there. The food's good, too.

Eric: I also want to find a shopping mall. I don't have any winter clothes. I'm from California.

Josh: One of (3. big/mall) .... is downtown. Just take the streetcar. I'll show you. It also has a gym.

Eric: Is it (4. good/gym) ....? I'm very serious about working out.

Josh: It's not the best, but it's one of (5. popular/gym) ....

Eric: Good. OK, one last thing. I need to register for a biology class. I need to pick (6. easy/professor) ....

Josh: None of the professors is easy. But Mr. Swan is (7. friendly) ....

C Imagine that you are giving advice to a new student in your area. Write five sentences about activities and places you recommend. Use superlative adjectives + nouns.

Ideas to write about:
- Places to meet people
- Cheap places to eat
- Good places to go shopping
- A popular gym
- Interesting classes to take

....

....

....

....

....

Lessons 34–37

Review

Too and *Enough*, Comparative and Superlative Adjectives

A Dictation Jason is thinking about talking to his wife about their next vacation. Write what you hear. Key words: *Coast Island, Santa Costa, energetic*

I need to talk to Amy about our vacation.

B Jason and Amy are thinking about where to go on vacation. Look at the information on three places they are considering. Use the information to complete the sentences on the next page. Sometimes more than one answer is possible.

	Santa Costa	Coast Island	Vista Coast
Money we have for our trip	$3000	$3000	$3000
Price of trip	$3100	$3500	$2600
Distance from here	2000 miles	2300 miles	500 miles
Length of flight	8 hours	10 hours	3 hours
Weather	sunny, warm	cloudy, warm	hot, humid, rainy
Drinking water	safe, clean	drink bottled	drink bottled
Number of clubs	10	10	6
Entertainment	a lot	a lot	a little
Beaches	very beautiful	beautiful	OK
Interesting place?	so-so	so-so	very

112

1. *as* + adjective + *as*   OR   *as* + *much/many* + *as*

distance   a. Coast Island is almost ___as close as___ Santa Costa.

weather   b. Santa Costa is _____ Coast Island.

clubs   c. Coast Island has _____ Santa Costa.

entertainment   d. Santa Costa has _____ Coast Island.

price   e. Vista Coast isn't _____ Coast Island.

2. *too* (+ adjective)   OR   *very*

a. They think the trip to Coast Island is _____, so they can't go there.

b. The weather in Vista Coast is _____ hot, but maybe they'll go there.

c. Vista Coast is _____ interesting, and they want to see the sights.

d. Jason says the flight to Coast Island is _____.

3. adjective + *enough*   OR   *enough* + noun

a. The water in Vista Coast isn't _____ to drink.

b. They like to go out at night. There isn't _____ in Vista Coast.

c. They don't have _____ to go to Coast Island, but they have almost _____ to go to Santa Costa.

4. **Comparative Adjectives:** adjective + *-er* + *than*   OR   *more* + adjective + *than*

price   a. The trip to Coast Island is _____ the trip to Vista Coast.

weather   b. The weather in Santa Costa is _____ the weather in Vista Coast.

weather   c. The weather in Vista Coast is _____ the weather on Coast Island

distance   d. Santa Costa is _____ Vista Coast.

water   e. The drinking water in Santa Costa is _____ the water on Coast Island.

beaches   f. The Santa Costa beaches are _____ the beaches on Coast Island.

5. **Superlative Adjectives:** *the* + adjective + *-est*   OR   *the most* + adjective

price   a. The trip to Coast Island is _____.

distance   b. Coast Island is _____ from here.

flight   c. _____ flight is to Coast Island.

weather   d. Vista Coast has _____ weather.

clubs   e. Vista Coast has _____ clubs.

beaches   f. Santa Costa has _____ beaches.

Have Fun

A Unscramble the letters to create comparative and superlative adjectives. Then use the numbered letters to find the secret message.

Irregular Comparative and Superlative Adjectives

1. EEBTRT — b e t t e r

2. TSBE — [ ][s][ ]
   (3)

3. EATHRFR — [f][ ][ ][ ][ ][ ]
   (7)

4. RAHTTFSE — [ ][ ][ ][ ][ ][ ][t]
   (9)

5. ESWRO — [ ][o][ ][ ]

6. RWOTS — [ ][ ][s][ ]
   (2)

7. ESLE — [ ][ ][s]
   (10)

8. LASTE — [l][ ][ ][ ]

Comparative Adjectives (-er)

9. DSADRE — [ ][d][ ][ ]
   (8)

10. TOEHRT — [ ][o][ ][ ][ ]
    (1)

11. RIGEGB — [ ][g][ ][ ]

12. NIISERO — [ ][i][ ][ ][ ]
    (11)

13. IERAES — [a][ ][ ][ ]

Superlative Adjectives (-est)

14. DLSTCEO — [ ][l][ ][ ]
    (6)

15. SADETDS — [ ][d][ ][ ]
    (5)

16. FTSUIENN — [ ][n][ ][ ][ ]
    (4)

17. HLTAESHIET — [ ][ ][ ][h][ ][ ]

18. TNESWE — [ ][w][ ][ ]

My [1][2] m [3] [4][5]
my [6][7][8][9][10][11].

114

B Spelling Bee Stand in a line with your classmates. Your teacher will say an adjective and ask for the comparative or superlative form. One by one, students will spell the words the teacher gives them. When students make mistakes, they will sit down. The last student spelling an adjective correctly is the winner.

C Chant

Her Worst School Year

She's not as smart as her mother.
She took the worst room on the floor.
She found the most difficult roommate.
She brought in enough luggage for four.
Her old room was much less expensive,
And it had a much nicer view.
Her roommate last year
Was smarter than this one
And always had fun things to do.
It's one of the best schools in the States,
But she's taking courses she really hates.
She's not as smart as her mother,
But this is her worst school year.

38 Past Continuous Tense—Affirmative and Negative Statements

The past continuous tense has two parts: **BE** and Verb + **ing**.

Use the past continuous tense to:
- talk about activities that were or weren't happening at a specific time in the past.
We were eating at the hotel last night at 7:00.   We weren't sleeping at 7:00.

- talk about two or more activities that were happening at the same time.
With **and**:   Jake was driving and Cecilia was taking pictures.
With **while**:   While Jake was driving, Cecilia was taking pictures.

- describe a scene when you tell a story.
The sun was shining. Many people were swimming in the clear, blue water of the lake.

In descriptions, you can use the past continuous tense with **There was/There were**.
There were many people swimming in the warm water.

Language Notes:
- When while comes at the beginning of a sentence, add a comma.
- When while comes in the middle of a sentence, don't add a comma.
- When you talk about one or more people doing more than one activity, it is not necessary to repeat the subject or was/were.   Cecilia was walking and taking pictures.
- Non-action verbs are not used in the past continuous tense. See Appendix E for a list of non-action verbs.

A Jake and Cecilia took a vacation last summer. Read about what they did. Underline the verbs in the past continuous tense. Then listen.

Last summer, Jake and Cecilia Miller spent a week in the mountains. There were a lot of people lying on the beach by the lake. The sun was shining, and the water was clear blue. Everyone was swimming. But the Millers weren't having fun. They wanted some action. So, they rented a car to see the sights.

While they were driving along a narrow, curvy road, Cecilia was taking pictures, and Jake was looking for a station on the radio. He wasn't paying attention, and he hit a big hole in the road. He stopped the car immediately. When he got out to check the car, he saw that they had a flat tire. They were all alone. Cecilia was beginning to worry when a truck full of teenagers appeared. Luckily, they offered to help. While three of the teenagers were changing the tire, the others were stopping the other cars on the road.

Finally, the spare tire was on the car. Cecilia and Jake thanked the teenagers and drove back to their hotel. They were tired but ready for their next adventure.

B Jake and Cecilia write to their friends about what happened. Fill in the blanks with the past continuous form of the verb in parentheses.

Hi Greg,

We're having a great time on our vacation. But yesterday was a little scary. Cecilia (1. take) .....was taking.................... pictures and (2. talk) .... to me while I (3. drive) ...., so I (4. [not] pay attention) .... to the road. I hit a huge hole and got a flat tire. While I (5. try) .... to stop the car, Cecilia (6. scream) .... Luckily, some kids stopped to help. While I (7. help) .... the kids change the tire, Cecilia (8. cry) .... in the car. She's OK now, though.

See you soon, Jake

Hi Betty!

We're having a lot of fun, but yesterday we had an accident. We (9. explore) .... the mountains. Jake (10. drive) .... too fast and (11. look) .... for a radio station. He (12. [not] watch) .... the road, and he hit a huge hole. We got a flat tire. Some kids (13. drive) .... by and stopped to help us. While the kids (14. change) .... the tire, I (15. sit) .... calmly in the car. You know me. I don't really worry. I think Jake was really afraid. I hope the rest of the trip is better.

Love, Cecilia

C Chant

The Girl in Room 403

I was talking to Bob, and he was talking to me.
But he was thinking about the girl in room 403.
She's learning Spanish. She doesn't speak very well.
But she's staying here in the same hotel.
She's taking her Spanish class right at the pool.
The students are wearing bathing suits to school.
Yesterday she was looking at herself in the glass.
She was walking along slowly to her Spanish class.
I was watching Bob, but he wasn't watching me.
He was watching that girl from Room 403.

39

Past Continuous Tense—Yes-No and *Wh* Questions

Use **Yes-No** questions in the past continuous tense to find out if something was happening at a specific time in the past.

BE	Subject	Verb+ing	
Were	you/we/they	studying	for the test this morning?
Was	I/she/he/it	eating	around 9:00?

Use short answers to respond to **Yes-No** questions.

Were you having breakfast this morning?   Yes, I was.

Was the teacher buying books when you saw her?   No, she wasn't. She was talking to some students.

Ask **Wh** questions in the past continuous tense to get information about something that was happening.

Wh Questions	Short Answers
Who was Ana eating with at 9:00?	Jon.
Where was Ana eating breakfast?	In the cafeteria.
Why was Chen studying for the test this morning?	Because he wanted a good grade.
When was Jon talking to his wife?	At noon.
What was Lily doing at 9:00?	Walking across the campus.

A Four students are talking about their missing teacher, Ms. Kelly. Read the questions. Then listen to the conversation and circle **Yes** or **No**.

1. Was Lily walking across campus at 9:00?   (Yes)   No

2. Was Ana studying at the library at 9:00?   Yes   No

3. Was the teacher walking into the cafeteria at 9:30?   Yes   No

4. Was Singh eating in the cafeteria at 10:30?   Yes   No

5. Was Chen studying for the test in an empty classroom?   Yes   No

6. Was Ms. Kelly walking across campus at 11:00?   Yes   No

B Write a question for each answer. Use the past continuous tense.

1. Was Ana eating in the cafeteria with Jon at 9:00?

Yes, she was eating in the cafeteria at 9:00.

2. What _____ at 9:00.?

Jon was talking to Ana at 9:00.

3. Why _____ for the test?

Chen was studying for the test because he was worried about getting a good grade.

4. Was _____ in the library?

No, Jorge wasn't studying in the library.

5. Where _____ lunch?

Jorge was eating lunch in the cafeteria at 12:00.

6. Was _____?

Yes, Ming was registering for a new class at 9:30.

7. When _____ in the campus pool?

Hoon was swimming in the campus pool at 10:30.

C Look at the two pictures. With a partner, ask and answer questions about what was happening at 11:30.

EXAMPLE   *Q: What was Navdeep doing at 11:30?*
          A: She was reading her textbook.

119

LESSON 40

Contrast: Past vs. Past Continuous Tenses

Don't use the past continuous tense with non-action verbs.

Use the past tense to talk about something that started and ended in the past.

Daniel's father **stopped** the band.

Daniel's father **raised** his glass and **made** a toast.

Use the past continuous tense to talk about:

• something that was happening at a specific time in the past.

At 7:30, everyone **was sitting** and **waiting**.

• two or more activities that were happening at the same time in the past.

While Daniel **was walking** down the aisle, his parents **were crying**.

Use the past continuous and past tenses together in a sentence to talk about a long action that was interrupted by a short action.

Use **while** + past continuous to show the longer action.
Use **when** + past tense to show the shorter action that interrupts the longer action.

longer action	shorter action
While they **were dancing,**	Daniels' father **stopped** the band.*

shorter action	longer action
Daniel's father **stopped** the band	while they **were dancing**.

*Use a comma only if the clause with **while** comes first in the sentence.

A Susan and Daniel got married last Saturday. Listen and write the missing word(s) in the blanks.

Susan and Daniel's wedding was last Saturday night. At 7:30, everyone (1.) _____ and (2.) _____ for the bride and groom. Finally, they (3.) _____ in. While Daniel (4.) _____ down the aisle, his parents (5.) _____.

After the ceremony, everyone (6.) _____ into the reception hall. While they (7.) _____, Daniel's father (8.) _____ the band because he (9.) _____ to make a toast. When the room was quiet, everyone (10.) _____ at the couple. Daniel's father (11.) _____ his glass and (12.) _____ the newlyweds a long, happy, and healthy life together. Everyone (13.) _____ up their glasses and (14.) _____, "I'll drink to that!"

B Susan and Daniel are in Hawaii on their honeymoon, and they just witnessed a car accident. A police officer is asking them what they saw. Fill in each blank with the past or past continuous form of the words in parentheses. (PO = police officer)

PO: (1. you/see) _Did you see_ the accident?

Daniel: Yes, we did.

PO: What (2. you/do) _____ when the accident (3. happen) _____?

Susan: We (4. buy) _____ a newspaper when we (5. see) _____ it happen.

PO: What (6. you/see) _____?

Daniel: Well, at about 1:45, that woman over there

        (7. cross) _____ the street. She

        (8. carry) _____ a heavy bag and

        (9. walk) _____ very slowly. The man in

        the black car (10. wait) _____ for her to

        cross the street.

PO: What happened then?

Daniel: The white car suddenly (11. come) _____ out of

        nowhere, and (12. hit) _____ the back of the black

        car. There (13. be) _____ a small explosion, and

        the black car (14. start) _____ to burn. Both drivers

        (15. jump) _____ out of their cars. Luckily the car

        (16. stop) _____ burning quickly.

PO: (17. you/see) _____ anything else?

Daniel: No, that's about everything.

PO: Thank you. You've been very helpful.

C Watch a few minutes of a videotape. In groups of three, write as many sentences as you can about what you saw. Write for five minutes. Use the past and past continuous tenses. Use **when** and **while** in at least two of your sentences.

EXAMPLE: _While the detective was driving, his cell phone rang._

Review
Past Continuous Tense

A **Dictation** Listen to the story about a scary night in a hotel. Write what you hear. Key words: *guests, lightening, struck, clerk, Mr. Chambers*

It was a dark and stormy night.

B (1.) Look at the dictation. Underline the verbs in the past tense. Circle the verbs in the past continuous tense.

(2.) What are three non-action verbs in the dictation?

(3.) Which sentence shows *action* (A) and which shows *non-action* (NA)?

_____ Everyone *looked* worried.   _____ Everyone *was looking* at him.

C With a partner, add to the story in Exercise A. Write four sentences in the past and past continuous tenses.

D Continue the story in the dictation. Fill in the blanks with verbs in the past or past continuous tense.

Doctor: He'll be OK. Just let him rest.

Clerk: It was terrible. I (1. read) _was reading_ at my desk and

everything (2. be) _____ fine. The guests (3. talk)

_____ and (4. drink) _____ tea by the fire.

Then, when I (5. hear) _____ the loud knock at the door,

I almost (6. fall out of) _____ my chair! I (7. run)

_____ to the door and (8. see) _____ that

young man. He (9. [not] be) _____ very friendly. He

(10. come) _____ in and (11. say) _____

he wanted to speak to Mr. Chambers. Poor Mr. Chambers. He (12. be)

_____ so shocked when he (13. see) _____

that young man. And I still don't know why!

E Ask five classmates questions with verbs in the past continuous tense. If a classmate answers, "Yes," put an **X** under "Yes, I was." If he or she answers, "No," write what they were doing.

EXAMPLE: Q: *Were you* _____ *at* _____?
                                      (activity)   (time)

A: *Yes, I was.*

OR: *No, I wasn't. I was* _____.

Activity	Time	Name	"Yes, I was."	"No, I wasn't. "	
doing homework	6:00 o'clock last night	Mariko		X	I was cooking dinner.
taking a nap	4:00 o'clock in the afternoon				
going to work	8:30 yesterday morning				
watching TV	9:00 last night				
visiting friends	3:00 yesterday afternoon				
eating lunch	noon yesterday				

Have Fun

A Mystery Writing Join a group of four students. Write a story describing what was happening in the home of Mr. and Mrs. Christie in London between 8:30 and 9:00 p.m. on Sunday night.

   Use the past and past continuous tenses. Share your story with your class. Useful vocabulary: *a thief, thieves, a cradle, a dresser, a drawer, make a toast*

B Observation With a partner, leave your classroom and observe what people are doing around your school or campus. Take short notes. Then write ten sentences using the past continuous tense.

EXAMPLES *People were using the Internet in the computer lab.*
In the cafeteria, some students were eating and some were studying.
While I was standing outside the building, some students were smoking.

C Chant

Stories

While I was driving to San Jose,
I got a call from my brother Ray.
He was shouting in Spanish.
He was laughing, too.
He was telling a wonderful story about you.
  Why was he shouting?
I don't know why.
  Why was he laughing?
He's a funny guy.

When Joe was running down the hall,
He slipped and fell right into the wall.
He was walking with a beautiful cane last night,
but he was smiling, and I'm sure he'll be all right.
  Was he running fast?
    He was flying.
  Was he laughing?
    He wasn't crying.

Verbs + Gerunds

Gerunds are nouns that are made by adding **-ing** to the base form of a verb.

Use gerunds after certain verbs to talk about activities.

Verb	Verb + Gerund	Verb	Verb + Gerund
avoid	He avoids eating meat.	imagine	I can't imagine working out with weights.
consider	He should consider using the treadmill.	miss	I never miss exercising.
		put off	I put off exercising.
dislike	Did she dislike running?	recommend	I recommend walking.
don't mind	He doesn't mind helping.	suggest	I suggest watching less TV.
enjoy	They enjoy getting exercise.	Other verbs we can use with gerunds: feel like, postpone,
finish	She finished exercising.	practice, quit, stop	

Language Notes:

• Don't use the infinitive (**to** + base form of verb) after the verbs listed above.

Correct: Paula enjoys exercising.   **Incorrect:** ~~Paula enjoys to exercise.~~

• Don't confuse gerunds with the continuous form of the verb.

Present continuous tense (**BE** + ing):   I am exercising now.

Past continuous tense (**BE** + ing):   I was working at 6:00 last night.

A Paula wants to get in shape. She is asking about joining a gym. Read the conversation and underline each verb + gerund combination. Then listen.

Paula: Hi. I'm interested in a gym membership. A few months ago, my doctor <u>recommended getting</u> in shape and suggested going to a gym. I put off coming here, but finally, here I am!

Pete: Well, you're in the right place! What kind of exercise do you enjoy doing?

Paula: Well, none, actually. I always avoid exercising. I enjoy watching TV and reading.

Pete: Do you like to walk?

Paula: Well, I guess I don't mind walking. You know, a long time ago I used to jog.

Pete: That's great. Maybe you should consider using the treadmill.

Paula: Sounds good. Maybe I won't miss sitting around and watching TV after work!

B After her first year of going to the gym, Paula enjoys a new, healthier lifestyle. Change the following verbs into gerunds. Then complete each sentence below with a gerund.

get- _ting_   get up- ....   eat- ....
use- ....   live- ....   spend- ....
be- ....   watch- ....   take- ....
work out- ....

1. Paula enjoys ..._getting_............ exercise now. She loves her new lifestyle.

2. Paula avoids .... sweets and fatty foods.

3. She doesn't mind .... early to go to the gym.

4. She enjoys .... TV in the evenings.

5. Paula can't imagine .... without daily exercise.

6. She recommends .... the treadmill.

7. She dislikes .... too much time at the office.

8. She is considering .... an exercise class.

9. She doesn't miss .... lazy.

10. When she finishes ...., she takes a shower.

C Write six **Wh** and **yes-no** questions about exercise. Use verbs + gerunds from the chart on page 126. Then ask your partner the questions and write his or her answers.

Ex: A: What kind of exercise do you enjoy doing? B: I like walking and running.

....

....

....

....

....

....

....

42 Expressions with Verbs + -*ing*

Use verbs + **-ing** after certain expressions to talk about activities.

Expressions

have fun	Did you **have fun** swimm**ing**?
have a good/great time	I **had a good time** camp**ing** last weekend.
have trouble	Harry **had trouble** mak**ing** a fire in the rain.
have a hard time	What did you **have a hard time** do**ing** on the trip?
have (a) problem(s)	They **had a problem** cook**ing**.
	They **had problems** putt**ing** up the tent.
spend time	They **spend time** camp**ing**.

Don't use the infinitive (**to** + base form of verb) after the expressions listed above.
Correct: They're having fun swimming.   **Incorrect:** ~~They're having fun to swim.~~

Language Note:

When you are talking about spending time, you can use time expressions after **spend**: spend **an hour** reading, spend **all day** working, spend **all weekend** camping. Put these time expressions between the verb **spend** and the gerund:

Correct: I spent **two days** driving to Seattle.
Incorrect: ~~I spent driving to Seattle two days.~~

A Read the story about a camping trip. Underline all the expression + verb + *ing* combinations. Then listen.

THE CAMPING TRIP

Most of the Chang family <u>had a great time camping</u> last week, but poor Harry Chang had problems putting up the tent. He had fun reading the instructions and putting the poles in the ground. But after that, he had trouble holding up the tent while he worked. Then he had a hard time tying the tent to the poles. He spent two hours trying and trying. Finally, he decided to go for a swim.

B Look at the pictures. Complete each sentence using an expression from the chart on page 128 and the gerund form of the verb in parentheses.

1. The kids _are having a good time hiking_ (hike).

2. Mary _____ (pull) the cooler.

3. Mary _____ (catch) fish.

4. Harry _____ (fish).

5. The kids _____ (take down) the tent.

6. Harry _____ (read).

C On a separate piece of paper, write a paragraph about a family vacation or trip. Or, write about what you, your family, or your friends like to do for fun. Use expressions with gerunds.

EXAMPLE: Last weekend, my family went to visit relatives. We spent three hours driving to their house. We had a great time celebrating my cousin's birthday. My aunt and my mom spent all day cooking a delicious dinner. But in the evening, we had trouble going home . . .

Share your paragraph with a partner or group. Make a list of all the verb phrases and gerunds that you and other students used in the paragraphs.

Gerund Subjects

A gerund can be the subject of a sentence.

In a statement, the subject comes before the verb.
Use the **he/she/it** form of the verb with a gerund subject.

	Subject	Verb	
Gerund subject—one word:	Running	is	good exercise.
Gerund subject—phrase:	Studying in a quiet place	helps	you concentrate better.

In a **Yes-No** question, the subject comes after the main verb or between the helping verb and the main verb.

	Verb	Subject	
Gerund subject—one word:	Is	running good exercise?	

	Helping Verb	Subject		Main Verb
Gerund subject-phrase:	Does	studying in a quiet place	help	you?

Make a gerund subject negative by putting **Not** in front of the gerund form.
Not getting enough sleep is unhealthy.

Language Note:
Use **It** as a pronoun to replace a gerund subject.
Adjusting to college is difficult. It (adjusting to college) is difficult.

A Read the advice for community college students. Underline the gerund subjects and circle the verbs. Then listen.

Welcome to your first year at community college. During this orientation, we want to give you some helpful advice. Keeping up with your work is very important. If you get behind, it will be hard to get good grades. Also, not getting enough sleep can be a very serious problem. Planning your schedule carefully will help you find time to get enough sleep.

In addition, saving time for relaxation will help you do a good job at school. For instance, seeing a movie with friends is a perfect way to relax. Going to college doesn't mean that you never have fun.

Finally, joining a study group will help you study better. When students work together, they can help each other. Joining student groups can help you make new friends, as well. Adjusting to college life can be difficult, but if you follow these tips, it will be easier for you.

B Complete the sentences with the words in the parentheses. Use a gerund subject.

1. _Studying an hour or two every day_ (study/an hour or two/every day) is important.

2. _____ (not/get/a good night's sleep) will make it

difficult to remember what you study.

3. _____ (keep/your notes organized) saves time.

4. _____ (is/use/the study labs on campus) helpful?

5. _____ (take advantage of/student services) is important.

C Look at the activities in the chart. Circle **easy** or **difficult**. Then have a conversation with a partner and circle his or her answers in the chart.

EXAMPLE: *A: Is (activity)* _____ *easy or difficult for you?*
              B: It's (easy) (difficult).

Activities	You		Your Partner	
learning English	easy	difficult	easy	difficult
cooking	easy	difficult	easy	difficult
playing tennis	easy	difficult	easy	difficult
playing soccer	easy	difficult	easy	difficult
finding time to study	easy	difficult	easy	difficult
getting enough sleep	easy	difficult	easy	difficult
keeping up with homework	easy	difficult	easy	difficult
being organized	easy	difficult	easy	difficult

Write eight sentences about you and your partner. Follow the form in these sentences.
    Learning English is difficult for my partner and me.
    Learning English is difficult for me, but it is easy for my partner.

D Chant

Lots of Fun

Teaching is fun, studying is too.
I like being a teacher and a student, don't you?
Buying a house is hard to do,
But selling your house is difficult, too.
Leaving your country is very sad.
Saying goodbye makes you feel so bad,
But meeting new people is lots of fun.
Making new friends, one by one,
Walking around, sitting in the sun,
Learning a new language is lots of fun.

Adjectives with *-ing* and *-ed*

Some adjectives end in **-ing** or **-ed**:

-ing adjectives show a cause or reason for something.
-ed adjectives show an effect, a result, or someone's feelings about a situation.

CAUSE (-ING)	EFFECT (-ED)
Our conversation was interesting. ⟶	We were interested.
The party will be boring. ⟶	The children will be bored.
The games are exciting. ⟶	Everyone is excited.

Language Note:

Use **-ing** and **-ed** adjectives with **be**, **look**, **seem**, and **feel**.

The games were *interesting*.   The children seemed *interested*.
All the food looks *amazing*.   They don't feel *tired* now.

A Ana and Sarah are planning a neighborhood "get to know you" party. Read their conversation and choose the correct **-ing** or **-ed** adjective from each pair in parentheses. Then listen to their conversation to check your answers.

PIÑATA

Ana: How about Saturday for the party? People won't be (1. tired/tiring) from work.

Sarah: Perfect. You know, we need some (2. excited/exciting) activities for the kids so they won't be (3. bored/boring).

Ana: How about a piñata? They'll be (4. excited/exciting) to get candy and toys.

Sarah: Good idea! It'll be an (5. interested/interesting) party because our neighbors come from so many different countries.

Ana: True. It'll be great to get to know everyone, and it'll help us feel safer.

Sarah: Yeah, after those (6. frightened/frightening) robberies in the neighborhood last month, I'm (7. frightened/frightening) at night when my husband is away.

Ana: I know what you mean. We'll all feel so much more (8. relaxed/relaxing) when we get to know each other better. We can look out for each other.

B Ana is writing an email to her sister after the neighborhood party. Fill in the blanks with the **-ed** or **-ing** form of the word in parentheses.

Hi Cecilia,

We finally had our neighborhood street party last Sunday. It was an

(1. excite) ___exciting___ day! Many people brought delicious and

(2. interest) _____ food. The kids were (3. excite)

_____ by the piñata and music. I'm glad that none of them were

(4. bore) _____.

It took a lot of work to organize the party with Sarah, but the party was very

(5. relax) _____. Everyone sat around and talked, and I was

(6. surprise) _____ when I found out that there are people

from seven different countries on my block!

You know, I was nervous about our new neighborhood, but now I feel much

more (7. relax) _____. We have a great group of neighbors,

and I know we'll all watch out for each other. Now I'm not so (8. frighten)

_____ when Jorge works late.

You have to come visit us soon!

Love, Ana

C Use the adjectives in the box to write eight sentences about somewhere you went recently (a party, a movie, a park). Share your sentences with a partner.

tiring/tired	surprising/surprised	disappointing/disappointed
amazing/amazed	annoying/annoyed	embarrassing/embarrassed
interesting/interested	exciting/excited	relaxing/relaxed

EXAMPLE:
    I recently went on a relaxing vacation.
    I was tired when I arrived but not when I left.

_____

_____

_____

_____

_____

_____

_____

_____

LESSON 45

Contrast: *-ing* Forms

Words with **-ing** can be gerunds (nouns), adjectives, or parts of continuous verbs.

Gerunds (activities)

Subject
Working with children is Matt's dream.

                  Object
Annie recommends taking education classes.

Adjectives

                  Adjective
Computer science is a fascinating subject.

Continuous Verbs

	Subject	BE	V + ING	
Present Continuous Tense:	I	am	taking	a computer class now.
Past Continuous Tense:	I	was	working	for a software company.

 A Listen to Matt's letter to the newspaper advice column *Dear Annie*. Fill in each blank with the word or words you hear.

See the inside of the back cover for "-ing" spelling rules.

DEAR ANNIE

Dear Annie,

    I (1.) <u>'m attending</u> my last year of classes at my college. (2.) .... a job that I really like worries me. Last year, I (3.) .... part-time at a software company while I (4.) .... classes, but I wasn't happy. In fact, it was a very (5.) .... job. I realized that I like (6.) .... with people more. Currently, I (7.) .... a course called, "How to Teach Computer Literacy to Children." It's a very (8.) .... class, and I love (9.) .... with children. (10.) I .... if I should stay in school longer. (11.) .... to children is what I really want to do. Is it too late to change direction?

Confused College Student

134

B Put each word from Exercise A ending in **-ing** into the correct column of the chart.

Gerund Subjects	Gerund Objects (Write verb + gerund.)	Continuous Verbs	*-ing* Adjectives (Write adjective + noun.)
Finding	like working	am attending	boring job

C Annie is writing back to the confused student. Complete the sentences with a word or phrase from the box.

working with children	interesting	was attending
am writing	staying	are taking

Dear Confused College Student,

I (1.) _am writing_ to say, "Congratulations!" You solved your own problem without my help. I'm so glad that you (2.) _____ a class in computers and teaching. Now you know what you want to do in the future. I recommend (3.) _____ in school another year to take more classes in education. Last week, while I (4.) _____ a workshop, I learned that schools really need people like you. I am sure that you will have an

(5.) _____ career. (6.) _____ will be perfect for you.

Annie

D Write a letter asking for advice about your studies or job choices. Use all four forms of **-ing** (see Exercise B). Then, exchange letters with a partner and write a response to your partner's letter.

....

....

....

....

....

....

Review
Gerunds, Adjectives with *-ing* and *-ed*

A **Dictation** Listen to some job interview advice. Write what you hear. Key words: *ahead of time, make an impression, employer, employee, success*

At the end of a job interview, the interviewer usually asks if you have any questions.

PREPARING QUESTIONS FOR A JOB INTERVIEW

B Use the dictation from Exercise A to complete the chart.

Gerund Subject	Verb + Gerund	Adjective -ing -ed

C Read more advice about interviewing for a job. On the line before each **-ing** form, write **G** for gerund, **A** for adjective, or **PC** for present continuous tense.

(1. ....) Answering questions with, "yes" or "no" is not enough. (2. ....) Giving explanations and details is a good idea. Also, show that you are (3. ....) enjoying (4. ....) talking to the interviewer. Smile! Let the person know that you think the job sounds (5. ....) exciting. And have confidence. Imagine (6. ....) working there and (7. ....) being successful. Let the interviewer know that you don't mind (8. ....) working hard and that you consider (9. ....) working there a dream come true. And finally, when you are (10. ....) sitting in the interview chair, think positive thoughts!

D What advice can you give someone who is looking for a job? Work with a partner and write sentences with gerund subjects.

1. Preparing well for an interview will help you get the job.
2.
3.
4.
5.
6.

E On a separate piece of paper, answer these questions in complete sentences.

1. What do you have trouble doing?
2. What do you have a good time doing?
3. What do you spend a lot of time doing?
4. What do you spend time doing on Saturdays and Sundays?
5. What do you like doing on Saturday nights?
6. What do you avoid doing at home?

F Answer the questions with short notes. Then ask a partner the questions and write short notes. When you finish, write twelve sentences with **-ed/-ing** adjectives about you and your partner.

confused/confusing	surprised/surprising	disappointed/disappointing
amazed/amazing	annoyed/annoying	embarrassed/embarrassing

Questions	Your Answers	Your Partner's Answers
1. What is one thing about English that is *confusing* to you?		
2. Is anything about English *surprising* to you? If yes, what?		
3. In what situations are you often *embarrassed*?		
4. What do you think is the most *amazing* thing in the world?		
5. What movie, TV program, book or trip was *disappointing* to you? Why?		
6. In what situations are you *annoyed*?		

Have Fun

A **Questionnaire** Follow these steps: (1) Read the statements in the questionnaire and underline the gerunds. (2) Circle a number that indicates your feelings about the statements. (3) Join a small group of students and talk about why you agree or disagree with the statements. (4) One student from each group will tell the class about three to five interesting comments that students in their groups made.

EXAMPLE: *Two of us dislike asking for directions. We don't really have a problem asking for directions, but we usually have trouble understanding what the other person is saying!*

Questionnaire
How I feel about learning English

	True (I agree.)		False (I don't agree.)		
1. I like <u>speaking</u> English.	1	2	3	4	5
2. I dislike asking for help or directions.	1	2	3	4	5
3. I don't mind speaking in front of a big group.	1	2	3	4	5
4. I can't imagine giving a speech in English in front of 100 people.	1	2	3	4	5
5. I avoid speaking my native language in class.	1	2	3	4	5
6. I'm considering trying some computer programs to learn English.	1	2	3	4	5
7. I enjoy watching TV in English.	1	2	3	4	5
8. I have a good time doing my homework.	1	2	3	4	5
9. I usually spend a lot of time doing my homework.	1	2	3	4	5
10. I have a hard time remembering spelling rules.	1	2	3	4	5
11. I'm having a problem finding time to work on my English.	1	2	3	4	5
12. Understanding a book or movie in English is exciting.	1	2	3	4	5
13. Listening to music helps me learn vocabulary.	1	2	3	4	5
14. Watching TV is good for my English.	1	2	3	4	5
15. Being successful is important to me.	1	2	3	4	5

B Guessing Game Use some of the adjectives in the box to write three *true* sentences and one *false* sentence about an experience you had. Explain what happened and how you felt. Ask your partner to decide which sentence is *false*.

interested/interesting	bored/boring	excited/exciting	embarrassed/embarrassing
tired/tiring	relaxed/relaxing	surprised/surprising	frightened/frightening

Use this pattern in your sentences:

I was _____*ed*.   It was _____*ing*.

C Chant

Slow Walker, Fast Driver

Walking is great, but would you mind slowing down?
You're walking too fast for me.
I had a good time walking last week,
But I fell and hurt my knee.
    I'm sorry. The same thing happened to me,
    But walking is good for your knee.
I know fast walking is fun for you,
But slow walking's fun for me.
I'm a slow walker and I love picking flowers
On a country road by the sea.
    I like picking flowers but not while I'm walking.
    That's a little boring for me.
    Slow walking or slow driving
    Are not the sports for me.
    Speed is exciting. I love fast cars.
    The highway is the place for me.

Verbs + Infinitives and
Verbs + Objects + Infinitives

An infinitive = **to** + the base form of a verb.   He wants **to go**.

These verbs are often followed by an infinitive:

be able	can't wait	hope	need	promise	want
can/can't afford	expect	know how	plan	try	would like

More verbs: agree, decide, forget, offer, pretend, refuse, seem

---

Subject	**Verb**	**Infinitive**		In a series of infinitives, you don't need to repeat **to**. I want to travel, write, and relax.
I	planned	to study	law.	

These verbs are often followed by an object + an infinitive:

allow	convince	help*	permit	teach	want
ask	expect	need	remind	tell	warn

***Help** is often followed by an object and the base form. I **helped** him **clean**.
More verbs: advise, beg, invite, persuade, would like

Subject	**Verb**	**Object**	**Infinitive**	
Yoshi's mother	wanted	him	to study	medicine.

Language Notes:

• Don't change the verb after **to**.

Correct: She planned **to visit** the college.   **Incorrect:** ~~She planned to visited the college.~~

• Don't omit **to**.

Correct: Would you like **to travel**?   **Incorrect:** ~~Would you like travel?~~

• Don't confuse the infinitive **to** with the preposition **to**.

Infinitive: He wants **to go**.   **Preposition**: He went **to** college.

A Manuel and Yoshi are talking about what they plan to do after high school. Listen and fill in each blank with the infinitive you hear.

Manuel: High school's finally over! I can't wait (1.) _____*to start*_____ college in the fall. I want (2.) _____ quickly and go to medical school. I plan (3.) _____ a cure for cancer and teach people (4.) _____ healthy.

Yoshi: Are you crazy? School's over. We're finally free! I want (5.) _____ in Europe, make money, and travel to Africa. I hope (6.) _____ the world before I'm 25.

Manuel: How can you expect (7.) _____ happy with no college education and no career?

Yoshi: I need (8.) _____ free. That's what makes me happy.

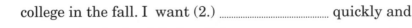

B Read the sentences about Yoshi. After each one, write a new sentence with a
similar idea. Use the verbs in parentheses with infinitives.

1. Yoshi is thinking about getting a job in Europe. (would like/work)

   Yoshi would like to work in Europe.

2. Yoshi doesn't have enough money to go to college. (can't afford/go)

   ....

3. Yoshi wants to visit Africa. (hope/travel)

   ....

4. Yoshi wants to go to Europe immediately. (can't wait/be free)

   ....

C Read the sentences about Manuel's parents. After each one, write a new
sentence with a similar idea. Use the verbs in parentheses with objects and
infinitives.

1. Manuel's parents think it's a good idea for him to go to medical school.
   (want/go)

   Manuel's parents want him to go to medical school.

2. Manuel's parents said he should be a responsible person. (tell/be)

   ....

3. Manuel can't pay for college by himself. His parents will help him.
   (need/pay)

   ....

4. Manuel's parents will give him some money for college. (help/pay)

   ....

D Chant

Dreams

She doesn't want to be a doctor.
She doesn't want to be a nurse.
She doesn't want to be the President.
She thinks there's nothing worse.
She would like to be an artist.
She hopes to study art.

She wants to move to Paris.
She knows how to follow her heart.
Her mother wants her to marry
And have a big family.
But she wants to go around the world
And paint the deep blue sea.

Infinitives after Adjectives

Use infinitives after some adjectives.

When a noun or a subject pronoun is the subject of the sentence, you can use these adjectives:

Noun/Pronoun	BE	Adjective	Infinitive	
I	am	lucky	to have	driving lessons.
Elsa	is	afraid	to drive	on narrow roads.
She	wasn't	ready	to go.	
We	were	happy	to go	to the beach.

More adjectives: disappointed, embarrassed, excited, glad, interesting, sad, surprised

When **it** is the subject, and it means the same thing as the infinitive in the sentence, you can use these adjectives:

	It	BE	Adjective	Infinitive	
	It*	wasn't	difficult	to learn	how to drive.
	It	is	important	to travel	safely.
Will	it	be	expensive	to rent	a car?

More adjectives: dangerous, easy, fun, hard, impossible, necessary

***It** = to learn

A Lena wants her teenaged friend Elsa to practice driving. Read their conversation. Circle the infinitives. Underline the adjectives that come before them. Then listen.

Lena: Let's go to the beach! You can practice your driving. My sister and her boyfriend can help you. You're <u>lucky</u> (to get) this opportunity.

Elsa: You know I'm afraid to drive that far.

Lena: Well, it's not really that far, and it's important to get a lot of practice.

Elsa: I don't know. The roads to the beach are really narrow, and people drive so fast.

Lena: Yeah, that's true. But you're a really good driver already. Besides, it's impossible to get to the beach without a car, and I'm too young to get a license. If you practice now, we can go all the time.

Elsa: You're right, I am a good driver. And it will be fun to practice with your sister. Let's do it!

B For each of the following sentences, circle the correct subject. Then use the past tense of **BE** with the words in the parentheses to complete each sentence. Use the pattern **BE + Adjective + Infinitive**.

1. It/(Elsa) (afraid/practice) ....was afraid to practice.......... driving too far.
2. They/It (fun/swim) .... in the ocean.
3. It/Lena (not easy/drive) .... on narrow roads.
4. Elsa/It (not excited/drive) .... on narrow roads.
5. It/They (lucky/find) .... a parking space.
6. Lena and Elsa/It (glad/walk) .... on the beach.
7. Elsa/It (not afraid/swim) .... in the ocean.
8. It/They (expensive/eat) .... at the restaurant.
9. They/It (easy/get) .... lost.
10. It/They (ready/go) .... home at the end of the day.

C Answer the questions about driving in complete sentences with adjectives + infinitives. Write your own question for number 5. Then ask a classmate the questions and write sentences about him or her.

EXAMPLE: I'm always happy to be the driver because I like to drive.
My partner isn't happy to be the driver because he likes to
relax and give the responsibility to someone else.

How do you feel about driving?	You	Your partner
1. If you have a driver's license, are you happy to be the driver when you go out with other people? Why or why not?		
2. Do you think it is necessary to learn to drive in today's world?		
3. Are you afraid to drive on the highway?		
4. Do you think it is difficult to drive in traffic?		
5.		

Infinitives of Purpose

Use infinitives to show purpose, to express the reason for an action.

Infinitives of purpose answer the question, "Why?"
A: Why did you come to the United States?
B: I came here to learn English.

Infinitives of purpose mean the same thing as **in order to**.
A: Why are you studying business?
B: I'm studying business to work in my father's company.
= I'm studying business in order to work in my father's company.

An infinitive of purpose can come at the beginning of a sentence.
It is separated from the main sentence by a comma.
To find a good job in the United States, you have to speak English very well.

Language Note:
Don't use **for** or **for + to** instead of an infinitive when you want to express purpose.
Correct: I came to the U.S. to go to the university.
Incorrect: ~~I came to the U.S. for go to the university.~~
Incorrect: ~~I came to the U.S. for to go to the university.~~

A Listen to the conversation between students Jin and Yuko. Match the infinitive of purpose on the right with the correct phrase on the left.

REASON (infinitive of purpose)

_b_ **1.** Jin came here

.... **2.** Jin's mother came here

.... **3.** Yuko came here

.... **4.** Yuko's father sent her to good schools in Japan

.... **5.** Jin needs to learn English

a. to live here.

b. to be with her family.

c. to learn English and go to a university.

d. to take care of her grandchildren.

e. to get a good education.

B Look at the underlined infinitives in each of the following sentences. Decide whether or not they are infinitives of purpose. (Ask yourself, "Does the infinitive give a reason for doing something?")

	Infinitive of Purpose?
1. Jin came to the U.S. <u>to make her mother happy</u>.	(Yes) No
2. Jin came here <u>to be with her family</u>.	Yes No
3. Jin's mother came here <u>to take care of her grandchildren</u>.	Yes No
4. Yuko came to the U.S. <u>to get a university degree</u>.	Yes No
5. Yuko likes <u>to study business</u>.	Yes No
6. Jin hopes <u>to get a good job</u>.	Yes No
7. Yuko will go back to Japan <u>to work</u>.	Yes No

C Answer each of the following questions using an infinitive of purpose. Write your answers on the first line. Circle the infinitive. Then ask a partner the same questions and write their answers on the second line.

1. Why do people move to another country?

   Many people move to another country (to find) a better job. ....

   ....

2. Why are you taking this class?

   ....

   ....

3. Why do people get regular exercise?

   ....

   ....

4. Why do people travel to other countries?

   ....

   ....

5. Why do people sometimes change jobs?

   ....

   ....

6. Why do people take vacations?

   ....

   ....

LESSON

49 Verb + Infinitive or Gerund

Use some verbs with gerunds *OR* infinitives.

| begin | continue | like | prefer |
| can't stand | hate | love | start |

Gerunds	**Infinitives**
I love going to the movies.	I love to go to the movies.
I'm going to start looking for a job.	I'm going to start to look for a job.

Language Note:

Hate and **can't stand** are very strong words. Be careful when you use them.

A Alex and Tan are waiting in line with their kids at the movies. Listen to the conversation and circle the gerund or infinitive that you hear.

Alex: This line is so long. I don't like (1. to wait/waiting) in long lines. I especially can't stand (2. to be/being) in line when it's so cold!

Tan: I know what you mean, but I really love (3. to see/seeing) movies.

Alex: Not me, I'm here for my kids. I prefer (4. to read/reading).

Tan: Really? I love (5. to go/going) to the movies, especially action movies. But my wife told me that I can't continue (6. to take/taking) the kids to those movies.

Alex: Why not?

Tan: Because they're so violent. She hates (7. to let/letting) the kids see all that violence.

Alex: She's right. I like (8. to take/taking) my kids to comedies. They won't have nightmares.

Tan: Oh look—the line started (9. to move/moving). Finally!

146

B Complete each sentence with a gerund or infinitive. Use your imagination. More than one answer is possible.

About movies:

1. Tan likes   _to go to action movies._

2. He doesn't like ....

About music:

3. Tan likes ....

4. His children don't like ....

About sports:

5. Tan's wife loves ....

6. Alex's wife doesn't like ....

About food:

7. Alex's kids hate ....

8. Tan's kids can't stand ....

About Alex and Tan:

9. Alex is going to begin ....

10. Tan is going to continue ....

C Write ten sentences about what kinds of movies, music, sports, or food you like and don't like. Use the following verbs with gerunds or infinitives: **like**, **love**, **hate**, **can't stand**, **prefer**. Share your sentences with a partner.

POSSIBLE FIRST SENTENCE: _I like going to some kinds of movies, but not all._

....

....

....

....

....

....

....

....

....

Review
Gerunds and Infinitives

A **Dictation** Toby is using an online dating service to find a girlfriend. Write what you hear. Underline the infinitives and circle the gerunds.
Key words: *Nicole, break up, once in a while*

Toby is using Get-A-Date.com
....
....
....
....
....
....

B Look at the dictation from Exercise A and use the information to complete the chart.

Verb + Infinitive	Verb + Object + Infinitive	Infinitive of Purpose	Verb + Gerund	Adjective + Infinitive
....	....	....	....	....
....			....	....
				....

C On a separate piece of paper, answer these questions about the dictation. Write complete sentences using the forms in Exercise B.

1. Why is Toby using Get-A-Date.com?
   Toby is using Get-a-Date.Com to look for a girlfriend.

2. What happened after six months?

3. Why do they have dinner once in a while?

4. Who wants Toby to get married?

5. What is he trying to do?

6. When did he begin looking?

7. What will he continue to do?

D Fill in each blank with an infinitive or gerund form of the verb in parentheses.

Nicole is ready (1. get) _____to get_____ married. She wants (2. ask) _____

Danny (3. marry) _____ her. But she expects him (4. say) _____,

"No" because he's afraid (5. get) _____ married.

Nicole visited her sister (6. get) _____ advice. Her sister told her

(7. be) _____ patient and wait. She told her (8. enjoy) _____

(9. be) _____ with Danny right now, and she suggested (10. wait)

_____ a few months before talking more about marriage.

That's going to be hard (11. do) _____. Nicole has trouble (12. keep)

_____ her feelings inside. She decided (13. talk) _____ to her old

boyfriend, Toby, about this (14. get) _____ his advice.

E On a separate piece of paper, give five pieces of advice to Nicole, and five pieces of advice to Danny. Then role play. Choose two students to be Nicole and Danny. Give them advice, and see what they say in response.

EXAMPLE: *Nicole, I recommend waiting. Don't ask Danny to get married right now.*

F Find the mistakes. Make the corrections. (One sentence is correct.)

1. Can you imagine ~~to use~~ a service like this? *using*

2. Some people postpone to get married, and then they are in a hurry to find someone.

3. Some people don't recommend using a dating service.

4. They suggest to meet people through friends.

5. Even some people in their 70s know how use online dating services.

6. Some services are expensive use, and some are free.

7. People use these services for to meet others.

8. She doesn't want to meets people this way.

9. Some people are able using online dating successfully.

10. Do you plan using this kind of service?

149

Have Fun

A Matchmaking

Step 1: Write ten sentences with verbs + infinitives or gerunds, verbs + objects + infinitives, and adjectives + infinitives. Use words from the box below.
Student A: Your sentences will be about the women, Laura and Nancy.
Student B: Your sentences will be about the men, Toby and Andrew.

Step 2: Read your sentences to each other. See if any of the men and women in the pictures make a good match.

> **Verbs:** plan/need/want/would like/hope/can't wait/help/teach/expect/like/love/prefer/start
> **Adjectives:** lucky/afraid/happy/ready/fun

STUDENT A

Laura

Nancy

Laura loves to ski.

STUDENT B

Toby

Andrew

B Chant

She Went to Peru to Learn Spanish

She went to Peru to learn Spanish.
He went to Greece to learn Greek.
They were lucky to have good teachers.
They taught them to read and to speak.

Speaking English is easy,
But speaking it well is tough.
I want to have a good accent,
But I'm afraid I don't practice enough.

I'm happy to go to the movies.
I love to hear English at home.
I'm able to read the papers
And speak to my friends on the phone.

She's working to improve her Spanish.
He's working to improve his Greek.
I'm hoping to improve my English.
We're all trying to learn how to speak.

LESSON 50

Phrasal Verbs 1 (Separable)

Phrasal verbs include a verb and a small word such as: **in, on, up, down, over, out**. The small word is called a particle.

The particle can change the meaning of the verb.

I **put** my homework assignment in my bag.

I **put off** doing my homework until 11:00.

Many phrasal verbs can be separated by a noun or an object pronoun. They are *separable*.

		Object	
Not separated:	I didn't turn in	my homework.	
Separated (by a noun):	I didn't turn	my homework	in.
Separated (by a pronoun):	I didn't turn	it	in.

Language Note:

• When the object is a pronoun, it always goes between the two words of the phrasal verb.

Correct: I always look them up in a dictionary.

Incorrect: ~~I always look up them in a dictionary.~~

More separable phrasal verbs:

look over = review, check something   put off = do something later

find out = learn new information   make up (an assignment) = do an assignment that you missed

write down = take notes

A Read about Katrina. Underline the correct word from each pair in parentheses. Then listen to check your answers.

My name is Katrina, and I'm 44 years old. I have two jobs and take care of my family. I go to school at night to learn English. It's hard for me to do all of the work for class. I try to turn (1. <u>in</u>/out) my homework on time, but sometimes I hand it (2. on/in) late. I try not to miss class because I know the teacher always passes (3. in/out) handouts, and I want to be there when she hands (4. it/them) out. I also need to be there to write (5. on/down) important information.

I'm always tired in class. Sometimes I don't understand the grammar lesson, and I have to figure it (6. on/out) at home. I look (7. out/up) new words in the dictionary, and sometimes I ask my son Frank to help me.

B Katrina is asking her other son Tom about school. Complete the conversation by writing questions and answers. Use nouns in the questions and pronouns in the answers.

Katrina: Tom, did you turn in your homework?

Tom: (1.) _Yes, Mom. I turned it in._

Katrina: (2.) _____ ?

Tom :   Yes, Mom. I figured out my math problems.

Katrina: Did you make up your English assignment?

Tom :   (3.) _No, Mom._

Katrina: (4.) _____ ?

Tom :   Yes, Mom. The teacher passed out the new science assignment.

Katrina: Are you putting off writing your paper?

Tom :   (5.) _No, Mom._

Katrina: Are you going to look up the addresses for the colleges you want to apply to?

Tom: (6.) _Yes, Mom._

C Write six sentences about your study habits when you were a younger student. Then write six sentences about your study habits now. Use phrasal verbs in your sentences. Share your sentences with a partner or small group.

Then: *I used to always turn my homework in late.*

1. _____

2. _____

3. _____

4. _____

5. _____

6. _____

Now: *I always turn it in on time.*

1. _____

2. _____

3. _____

4. _____

5. _____

6. _____

Phrasal Verbs 2 (Inseparable)

Some phrasal verbs are inseparable. The verb and the particle cannot be separated by an object.

Correct: The teacher called on Pablo to answer a question.
Incorrect: ~~The teacher called Pablo on to answer a question.~~

Some inseparable phrasal verbs have objects and some do not.

• Inseparable phrasal verbs that have objects:
call on (*a student*), **get in** (*a car*), **get off** (*a plane*), **get on** (*a bus*), **get along with** (*a friend*), **get over** (*a cold or a problem*), **look after** (*a child*), **run into** (*a friend*)

Carlos ran into his friends.   The teacher called on Pablo.

• Inseparable phrasal verbs that don't have objects:
come back, come over, drop by, eat out, fit in, get up, grow up, stay out

They stayed out all afternoon.   They came back around 7 o'clock.

A Pablo is spending a few months of elementary school with his friend Carlos in Arizona. Read the email from Carlos's mother to Pablo's mother. Complete the phrasal verbs by filling in each blank with the correct word. Listen to check your answers.

To: Fern@terra.mx   From: Maria@ariz.net
Subject: Pablo's doing fine.

Dear Fernanda,

Pablo's having a great time in Arizona. His first day of school was Monday. The boys got (1.) _up_ early. They got (2.) _____ the bus near our house, and Pablo learned where to get (3.) _____ the bus when he goes to school by himself. At school, the teacher called (4.) _____ Pablo twice, and he answered in English.

On Saturday, they ran (5.) _____ some of Carlos's friends, and the boys stayed (6.) _____ all day and played. The two boys came (7.) _____ around seven o'clock. Then we all ate (8.) _____ at our favorite pizzeria. When we came home, Carlos's cousin dropped (9.) _____, and the three of them listened to music and played computer games. Pablo will fit (10.) _____ well. Everyone seems to like him. I know I do!

  Maria

B Look again at the email in Exercise A. Write the phrasal verbs with no object in the chart on the left. Write phrasal verbs that have an object on the right. Include the object.

Phrasal Verb (no object)		Phrasal Verb (+ object)	
got up	....	*got on the bus*	....
....	....	....	....
....	....	....	....

C Pablo is talking to his mother Fernanda on the phone. Complete the conversation with forms of the phrasal verbs in the box. Use each verb only once.

| get over   come over   fit in   call on   come back   get on   look after |

Fernanda: Maria says you (1.) .... *fit in* .... very well. I'm so proud of you!

Pablo: It's OK here. But my teacher (2.) .... me a lot.

Fernanda: I know you don't like to talk in class. But when you (3.) .... to Mexico, you'll know English really well. Isn't that what you want?

Pablo: Yes, but I miss you and everyone. Mom, I want to (4.) .... a plane right now and fly home!

Fernanda: Oh, you're just a little homesick, Pablo. You'll (5.) .... it. Do you like spending time with Carlos?

Pablo: Sure. We have a great time. His friends (6.) .... a lot.

Fernanda: Well, that's great. And I know that Maria and Miguel (7.) .... you very well. You'll be fine.

D Chant

That's Life!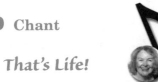

We got in a cab at eight.
We got to the airport at nine.
He got on a plane at ten,
And I never saw him again.

I dropped by the office
And ran into Joe.
He just got back from Mexico.

Gus was home in bed
Getting over the flu.
He said it felt great
To be ninety-two!

Verb + Preposition Combinations

Use prepositions after some verbs.

Verb + *about*	Verb + *to*	Verb + *in*	Verb + *on*
dream about	look forward to	participate in	concentrate on
think about	listen to	believe in	depend on
care about	talk to	succeed in*	
forget about			
talk about			

*You can also say succeed at.

(See Appendix I for more verb + preposition combinations.)

Don't confuse infinitives with verb + preposition combinations.

	Subject	Verb	Preposition	Noun or Gerund
Correct:	High school students	look forward	to	graduating.
Correct:	High school students	look forward	to	graduation.
Incorrect:	High school students	look forward	to	~~graduate.~~*

*The **to** in **look forward to** is a preposition. It is not the infinitive **to**:

She looks forward **to** graduation. (**to** + noun)

She wants to graduate. (**to graduate** = infinitive—to + base form of the verb **graduate**)

A Read the counselor's advice to high school seniors. Circle the verb and preposition combinations. Underline the nouns or gerunds that come after the prepositions. Then listen.

Do you dream about being out of high school? Do you look forward to being a college student or getting a job? Well, you're almost there.

This year, you have some important things to do. You should concentrate on getting good grades because it's time to think about applying to college. Talk about your college possibilities with your family. And talk to your teachers and counselors. We'll listen to you because we care about your future. You can depend on us to help you.

Also, don't forget about enjoying the senior activities. Try to participate in all of them. Most importantly, believe in yourself, and you'll succeed in reaching your goals.

B Write each of these verbs in the correct circle. Don't look at page 156.

dream
look forward
concentrate
succeed
care
listen
believe
depend
think
participate
forget
talk (use twice)

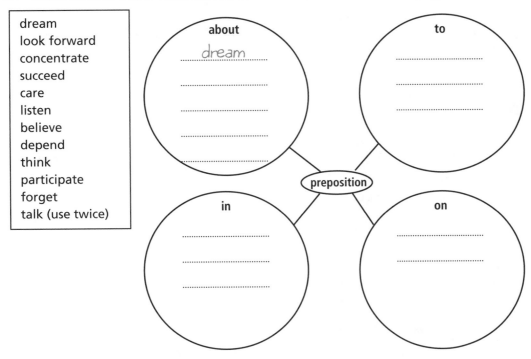

about
dream

to

preposition

in

on

C Add the correct preposition and a form of the words in parentheses to each of the following sentences. Make sure a noun or gerund comes after each preposition.

1. Many students are listening (the speech) _____to the speech._____

2. Some students look forward (go) _____ to college.

3. Their parents are dreaming (success) _____ for their children.

4. The kids want to succeed (get) _____ good grades.

5. They also want to participate (senior activities) _____

6. Some students are thinking (get) _____ advice.

D Interview two classmates about their lives when they were younger. Take notes on their experiences. Then write four sentences about each classmate.

When you were younger...	Classmate # 1	Classmate # 2
1. What did you care a lot about?		
2. What did you look forward to doing in the future?		
3. What did you think about doing after you finished school?		
4. What did you succeed in doing?		

Adjective + Preposition Combinations

See Appendix I for a list of more adjective + preposition combinations. See Lesson 5 for more information on prepositions.

Use prepositions after most adjectives.

Adjective+about	Adjective+of	Adjective+at	Adjective+in	Adjective+for
nervous about	capable of	good at	interested in	responsible for
excited about	proud of	bad at	successful in	famous for
sad about	afraid of	successful at		perfect for
happy about	tired of	surprised at (or surprised *by*)		late for

The verb **BE** is the most common verb we use with adjectives.

She **is** *responsible for* supervising her department.

Other verbs used with adjectives:

become **excited about**; get **nervous about**; feel **proud of**; seem **capable of**

Don't use an infinitive or base form after a preposition.

	Subject	Verb	Adjective	Preposition	Noun or Gerund
Correct:	Lucy	is	responsible	for	new employees.
Correct:	Lucy	is	responsible	for	training them.
Incorrect:	~~Lucy~~	~~is~~	~~responsible~~	~~for~~	~~to train them.~~
Incorrect:	~~Lucy~~	~~is~~	~~responsible~~	~~for~~	~~train them.~~

A Lucy is talking to her mother about changing jobs and moving to a new city. Write the correct preposition in each blank. Then listen to check your answers.

Lucy: Well, Mom, I'm all packed. I'm nervous (1.) _about_ going, but I'm excited (2.) _____ my new job.

Mom: What are you nervous about? You're capable (3.) _____ doing anything you want. I'm so proud (4.) _____ you. You'll be fine, and this job is perfect (5.) _____ you. You're really good (6.) _____ what you do.

Lucy: Thanks, Mom. I'm sad (7.) _____ leaving my friends, but I'm happy (8.) _____ this new opportunity. I know I'll meet new people, and I'm interested (9.) _____ learning about this new company. I'll be responsible (10.) _____ a lot.

Mom: You'll be great. Now let's go. There's a lot of traffic, and you don't want to be late (11.) _____ your flight.

B Write each of these adjectives in the correct circle. Don't look at page 158.

| afraid | perfect | tired | sad | successful (use twice) | responsible | famous |
| proud | interested | late | capable | excited | nervous | bad | good |

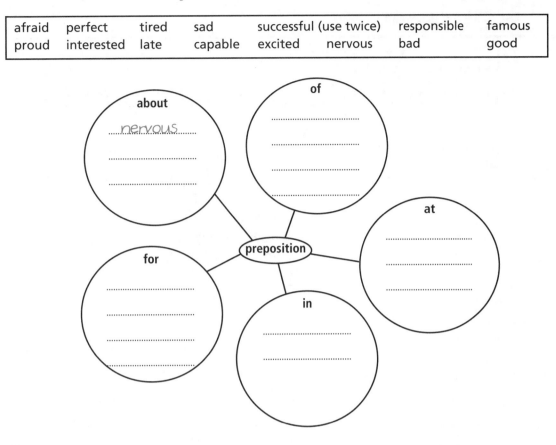

about
.....nervous......
....
....

of
....
....
....
....

at
....
....
....

for
....
....
....

in
....
....

preposition

C Add the correct preposition and a form of the words in parentheses to each of the following sentences. Make sure a noun or gerund comes after each preposition.

1. Lucy's boss says she's capable (do) _of doing_ .... a good job.

2. I'm not bad (supervise) .... people.

3. I'm surprised (the amount of work) ....

4. Lucy feels proud (herself) ....

5. She's becoming famous (be) .... a great cook.

6. The job seems perfect (her) ....

7. She isn't getting tired (work) .... hard.

D On a separate piece of paper, complete each of these sentences with information about you. Use prepositions + nouns or gerunds. Share your sentences with a partner or small group.

EXAMPLE: *I am capable **of taking** care of my family.*

1. I'm happy . . .

2. I'm (or I'm becoming) interested . . .

3. I'm not interested . . .

4. I'm getting tired . . .

5. I was nervous . . .

6. I feel proud . . .

7. I will be successful . . .

8. I wasn't afraid . . .

Review

Phrasal Verbs
Verbs and Adjectives + Prepositions

A **Dictation** Rosie is talking about being stuck on an elevator. Listen and write what you hear. Key words: *theater, anyway*

All day yesterday,

....

....

....

....

....

B On a separate piece of paper, answer each of these questions about the dictation from Exercise A. Write complete sentences.

1. What was Rosie looking forward to?

2. What was she planning to do before the show?

3. What was she surprised at?

4. What happened last week?

5. What is Rosie going to do?

C Fill in each blank in the paragraph about Rosie.

Rosie and her friend stayed (1.) ___out___ late. After the show, they went to a cafe for a snack and ran (2.) _____ Rosie's old boyfriend Norman. Rosie used to care (3.) _____ Norman a lot. When they broke up, she tried to forget (4.) _____ him, but it was hard. At first, Rosie was nervous (5.) _____ talking to him, but she relaxed after a while. Rosie and her friend talked (6.) _____ Norman for around an hour, and they were interested (7.) _____ hearing his news. While they were talking, Rosie suddenly realized that Norman was perfect (8.) _____ her friend.

D Find the mistakes. Make the corrections. (One sentence is correct.)

1. Everyone looked forward to ~~get~~ *getting* out of the elevator.

2. Everyone was interested to get off.

3. Some people took their cell phones out.

4. Their phones didn't work in the elevator, so they put away them.

5. She dropped her phone and someone picked up it.

6. The fire department succeeded getting everyone out safely.

7. They were responsible for to take care of everybody.

8. Rosie only cared about get to the theater on time.

9. She didn't eat out, but she wasn't late at the show.

10. At the theater, she didn't get it in the elevator. She walked up the stairs.

E **Find Someone Who** Complete the phrasal verbs with a particle. Then write questions to ask your classmates. Walk around and ask the questions. When classmates say, "Yes," write their first names on the lines.

Names of Students
who said "Yes"

1. eats ....*out*.... once a week

   Do you eat out once a week?   ....

2. ate .... last Saturday night

   ....

3. gets .... late on Sunday mornings

   ....

4. always turns homework .... on time

   ....

5. put .... studying for tests

   ....

6. usually writes .... what the teacher says

   ....

7. frequently drops .... friends' houses

   ....

161

Have Fun

A **Tic-Tac-Toe** Your teacher will put these games on the board. You will be on Team **X** or Team **O**. Follow the directions below for each game. Your team can talk about what to say for up to thirty seconds. Students should take turns giving the answers. The first team to get three Xs or Os in a straight line wins. The line can be horizontal (—), vertical (|), or diagonal (/) (\ ). Repeat the game with words from Lessons 51 and 52 and from Appendix I.

Game 1—Make sentences with phrasal verbs.

hand in	put off	make up
look over	call on	run into
drop by	pick up	look up

Game 2 — Add prepositions. Make sentences.

be responsible	capable	interested
look forward	care	succeed
dream	think	depend

B Bring in three pictures of people from magazines or newspapers. Get into small groups and talk about the people. Use phrasal verbs and verbs/adjectives + prepositions from Appendix I.

EXAMPLE:

This is Charlie. He always puts off cleaning his room.
His mother tells him to clean, but he doesn't listen to her.

C Chant

Good Friend

We look forward to seeing you in Boston.
We want to hear about your wonderful job.
I looked up the name of your company.
I think the President is my Uncle Bob.
I want to find out more about him.
I want to know his name.
I think I was at his wedding.
He married my dear Aunt Mame.
We're very happy to hear about your marriage.
We think about you and your wife.
You know we really care about you,
And we hope you'll have a wonderful life.

Could/May/Might (Possibility)

"Could" also means past ability: He could surf ten years ago, but he can't now. "May" is also used to ask for and give permission.

Could, **may**, and **might** are modals of possibility.

Use **could**, **may**, or **might** with the base form of a verb to talk about something that is possible in the present or future.

	Modal	Main Verb	
I don't know his occupation. He	could/may/might	be	a policeman.
I'm not sure. He	may not/might not	like	noise.
We should take an umbrella. It	could/may/might	rain	later.

Language Notes:

• Modals are the same for all subjects.

I/You/He/She/We/They could/may/might be a policeman.

• Don't add **-s** or **-ing** to main verbs that go with modals.

Correct: He may work at night.   **Incorrect:** ~~He may works at night.~~

                                          ~~He may working at night.~~

• Don't put the infinitive **to** after a modal.

Correct: He may work at night.   **Incorrect:** ~~He may to work at night.~~

A Listen to Rika and Jon talk about a mysterious neighbor. Circle the correct choice in the parentheses.

1. Rika (might have/(has)) a new neighbor.

2. Rika's new neighbor (is/could be) at work a lot.

3. He (is/might be) very busy.

4. He (could be/is) a doctor or a policeman.

5. He (keeps/might keep) his curtains closed.

6. He (doesn't open/might open) his windows in hot weather.

7. He (likes/may like) peace and quiet.

8. He (is/could be) 40 or 50.

9. He (has/might have) some gray hair.

B Find the mistakes. Make the corrections.

1. The new neighbor might works at night.

2. He could to be a doctor.

3. He may not has a job.

4. The new neighbor might to be a policeman.

5. He might not a doctor.

6. Rika and Jon may meeting him soon.

C Look at the information below. Work with a partner and write sentences about what you think Rika and Jon might do or be in the future.

RIKA

Major: computer science

Hobbies: travel, tennis, painting

Interests: working with children, dance competitions

JON

Major: biology

Hobbies: soccer, photography, writing poetry

Interests: helping sick people, working in a laboratory

Rika

1. Rika might teach children how to use computers.

2.

3.

4.

5.

6.

Jon

1.

2.

3.

4.

5.

6.

Must (Making Logical Conclusions)

Must is a modal.
Use **must** with the base form of a verb to make a guess or draw a conclusion based on evidence (something you know or see or what someone told you).

Evidence	Conclusion
The dog isn't too thin,	so he must eat well.
He seems like a puppy.	He must not be old.
Your dog is missing.	You must be worried.

Language Note:

Must has more than one meaning.

Necessity: We must eat in order to live.

Prohibition (something is not permitted/allowed): You must not smoke in the classroom.

Conclusion: The dog must eat well because he looks healthy.

A Listen to Rika and Jon talk about a mysterious dog. Circle the correct choice in the parentheses.

1. He (is/must be) well-trained.

2. He (must eat/eats) well.

3. He (likes/must like) kids.

4. Rika's sister and brother (want/must want) to keep the dog.

5. His owner (is/must be) very upset.

6. The dog (must belong/belongs) to someone else.

7. The dog (must not have/doesn't have) a name tag.

8. He (isn't/must not be) very old.

9. Rika (is thinking about/must be thinking about) putting up signs in the neighborhood.

B Fill in each blank with **must** or **must not** + a verb.

1. The dog looks tired. He ___*must not sleep*___ enough.

2. The dog looks very clean. Someone _____ care of him.

3. He acts very friendly. He _____ people.

4. He keeps looking out the window. He _____ homesick.

5. He's pretty big. He _____ a puppy.

6. He's running in circles. He _____ to play.

C Look at the pictures. For each one write an affirmative or negative sentence with **must** + the verb **be** or **like**. Share your sentences with a partner.

1.

The baby must be tired and hungry.

2. _____ _____

3. _____ _____

4. _____ _____

5. _____ _____

6. They _____ _____

LESSON 56

Should (Advice) and Have To (Necessity)

"Must" is similar to "have to." "Have to" is more common.

Should is a modal. Use **should** or **shouldn't** to give advice to someone.
Use **should** with the base form of a verb.
Use **I think** or **I don't think** when you are not sure or when you want to be polite.

(I Think/I Don't Think)	Subject	Should	Base Form
(I think) (I don't think)	I/you/he/she/we/they	should/shouldn't should	carry a lot of cash.

Use **have to/doesn't have to** to show that something is (not) necessary.

	Subject	Have To	Base Form
Present/Future Necessity	I/You/We/They He/She	have to/don't have to has to/doesn't have to	get a visa. get a visa.
Past Necessity	I/You/He/She/We/They	had to/didn't have to	bring an ATM card.

A Read about Francisco, who is going to visit relatives in Argentina. Underline the correct answer from each pair in parentheses. Then listen to check your answers.

Francisco was born in the United States. Next month he's going to visit Argentina for the first time. Francisco's parents are from Argentina, and he wants to meet his relatives. He's a little nervous because he has a lot to do before he goes. He (1. <u>has to</u>/doesn't have to) renew his passport for the trip because it expired, but he (2. doesn't have to/has to) get a visa. He doesn't need a visa to go to Argentina.

His mother told him that he (3. should/shouldn't) take gifts to his relatives because they like to get presents from the United States. It's winter in Argentina in July, so he (4. shouldn't/should) take summer clothes. He (5. has to/doesn't have to) take warm clothes. He (6. doesn't have to/has to) make hotel reservations because he can stay with relatives. His mom said he (7. should/shouldn't) take a lot of cash. Instead, he (8. should/shouldn't) take his ATM card. He knows he (9. should/shouldn't) go to bed early the night before the flight because it's a long trip.

168

B Complete each sentence with **should**, **shouldn't**, **have to**, **don't have to**, **had to** or **didn't have** to.

I'm Diego, Francisco's cousin. We had a great time last July when he visited Argentina, and now I'm planning to visit him in San Diego. He told me I (1.) _____should_____ visit him because he lives in a city with my name. Then I told him that we (2.) _____ take a trip to San Francisco because his name is Francisco!

Before I go, I need to work on my English. I signed up for an English class, but I missed the first class because I (3.) _____ work. When I went to the second class, the teacher gave me some advice. She said, "You (4.) _____ choose between work and school." Well, I (5.) _____ work to save money for my trip, so I decided to study English on my own.

There's a cafe in the city where people practice their English. Since I (6.) _____ work last Friday, I went and talked to a tourist from Los Angeles for about an hour. It was great! I asked her a lot about California. Now I know I (7.) _____ rent a car in San Diego because it's a big city, but I (8.) _____ rent a car in San Francisco because it's hard to park there.

C Chant

Good Advice

I think he should go.
I don't think he should stay.
But he doesn't have to make a decision today.
He should think about it.
He should take his time.
He doesn't have to hurry.
Waiting is not a crime.

I want him to stay right here by the sea.
But he has to go to work. Don't you agree?
You shouldn't be nervous.
You shouldn't feel bad.
But he has to leave soon,
And you shouldn't feel sad.

Questions with *Should* and *Have To*

Use **should** to ask for advice.

Yes-No Questions with *Should*

Should	Subject	Base Form	Short Answer
Should	I/you/she/he/we/they	sign a lease?	Yes, you should. No, you shouldn't.

Use **have to** to ask if something is necessary.

Yes-No Questions with *Have To*

	Subject	Have to	Base Form	Short Answer
Do	I/you/we/they	have to	pay a deposit?	Yes, we do. No, we don't.
Does	she/he	have to	pay a deposit?	Yes, she does. No, she doesn't.

Wh Questions	Answers
When **should** we move in?	Next weekend.
What **should** we do before we move in?	Paint the house.
When do they **have to** sign the lease?	Tomorrow.
Where do they **have to** meet the landlord?	In his office.

A Carol and Mike are discussing their new house and the things they need to do before they can move in. Listen to the conversation and circle **now** or **later** next to each question about Carol and Mike's situation.

1. When do they have to buy a new stove?	(Now)	Later
2. When should they buy a new refrigerator?	Now	Later
3. When should they paint the outside of the house?	Now	Later
4. When should they paint the inside of the house?	Now	Later
5. When do they have to buy new windows?	Now	Later
6. When do they have to buy a new bed?	Now	Later
7. When do they have to fix the roof?	Now	Later

B Carol and Mike's son Jim is moving into a new apartment. Use each set of words in parentheses to write a **yes-no** or **Wh** question to go with an answer on the right.

Questions	Answers
1. (what type/lease/sign)	
What type of lease does Jim have to sign?	He has to sign a one-year lease.
2. (call the cable company to connect his TV)	
....	Yes, he should.
3. (when/change his address)	
....	He should change it soon.
4. (pay a deposit)	
....	No, he doesn't have to.
5. (what/furniture/buy)	
....	He has to buy a bed and a couch.
6. (where/look for a truck to rent)	
....	He should look online.
7. (reserve/a truck)	
....	Yes, he should.

C Write questions you would ask a teacher on the first day of school. Then role play with a partner. One of you will be a student and the other will be the teacher. Take turns asking and answering questions. Write your partner's answers on the right.

EXAMPLE: *Should we bring a dictionary to class?*

Questions	Your "Teacher's" Answers
1. Should	
2. Do (have to)	
3. When should	
4. What should	
5. Where should	

171

The Base Form of a Verb

The base form of a verb has no -**s**, no -**ed**, and no -**ing**.
Verbs are listed in their base form in the dictionary.

Use the base form:

• in negative statements and questions that have helping verbs.

Present Tense
He doesn't **teach** gymnastics.
Does she **have** a photo of them?

Past Tense
He didn't **own** a gym before.
Did she **graduate**?

Correct:	He doesn't play.	Does he like it?	Did he play?
Incorrect:	~~He doesn't plays.~~	~~Does he likes it?~~	~~Did he played?~~

• with **will/won't**.

He will **play** soccer.   He won't **play** basketball.   Will he **play** basketball?

• after verb + **to** (infinitive) and after adjective + **to** (infinitive).

Correct: He wanted to **play**.   **Incorrect:** ~~He wanted to played.~~

Correct: I was happy to **see** you.   **Incorrect:** ~~I was happy to saw you.~~

• after **can, could, should,** and other modals. Don't use **to** after modals.

Correct: He can **go**.   **Incorrect:** ~~He can to go.~~

• after **used to**.

Correct: He **used to** play soccer.   **Incorrect:** ~~He used to playing soccer.~~

Language Notes:
Don't use the base form after am/is/are/was/were: ~~He is live here.~~   ~~He was go.~~
Don't use the base form after **he**, **she**, **it**.   ~~He go.~~

A Read Tran and Susana's conversation. Underline the correct verb in the parentheses. Not all verbs are in the base form. Then listen to check your answers.

Tran: Hi, Susana. How are you? I'm so happy to (1. <u>see</u>/seeing) you!

Susana: Tran! You look great! What are you (2. do/doing) these days?

Tran: Well, you know, I used to (3. be/being) a gymnastics teacher. But last year I decided to (4. open/opened) my own gym.

Susana: Wow! That's terrific! I should (5. go/to go) to your gym. I need some exercise.

Tran: I hope you do! So, what's new with you? Did you (6. graduate/graduated)?

Susana: Yes, last month. Now I'm (7. look/looking) for a job in a hospital.

Tran: I'm sure you'll (8. get/to get) a job soon.

B Look again at Exercise A. Write a **yes-no** or **Wh** question for each of the following answers. Then circle the base form of the verb in each question. Sometimes there are two base forms in one question.

1. _Do Tran and Susana (know) each other?_

   Yes. They know each other from their English class.

2. What ....

   He decided to open his own gym.

3. What ....

   She wants to get a nursing job at a hospital.

4. ....

   Yes. He used to be a gymnastics teacher.

5. ....

   Yes, she should join his gym.

6. ....

   Because she needs some exercise.

C Find the mistakes in this conversation between Maki and Susana. Make the corrections. If a sentence is correct, write C.

1. Maki: Hi Susana. Where did you ~~went~~ *go* today?

2. Susana: Downtown. And guess what? I saw our old classmate Tran!

3. Maki: I remember Tran. He used to being a gymnastics teacher.

4. Susana: That's right. Well, last year he decided to opened his own

   business.

5 Maki: That's very exciting. Does he lives near here?

6. Susana: I don't know. I wanted to asked him that question, but I

   didn't had time.

7. Maki: I would like to see him.

8. Susana: Well, you can visit him at his new gym. It's downtown.

9. Maki: We should going together.

10. Susana: Good idea!

D Imagine it is three years from now. You run into an old friend from your English class. On a separate piece of paper, write an eight-line conversation between you and your classmate. Use **used to**, **will**, **should**, **decide to**, and **want to** in your conversation.

Possible first lines:

Mari: Hi Carolyn. How are you?

Carolyn: Hi Mari! It's good to see you. Do you want to get some coffee?

Review
Modals, Base Forms of Verbs

A **Dictation** Bob is new in his apartment building and he is throwing away garbage. His brother Bill walks up and gives him some advice.
Key words: *recycle, landlord, containers, Yup, shy, help out*

Bill: Hey, Bob! You shouldn't throw those newspapers away.

Bob: ....

Bill: ....

Bob: ....

Bill: ....

....

....

Bob: ....

B Find the mistakes. Make the corrections. (One sentence is correct.)

1. Does Bob ~~has~~ _have_ to recycle?
2. He used to recycling at his other apartment.
3. Where he should put the newspapers?
4. He have to help the environment.
5. Bill must cares about the environment.
6. Does he recycles glass too?
7. There might not a place to put the newspapers.
8. He had to cleaned his apartment.
9. He didn't had to help his brother.
10. He may look for his landlord later.
11. Bill can to help his brother.
12. Bill wants to helps Bob.
13. Bill was happy to helped Bob.

C For each picture, write a question and answer. Use **should, have to, must, could, may,** or **might**.

1.

Q: What's wrong?

A: He must be late for class.

2.

A student?

A teacher?

Q: What is he?

A: ....
....

3.

Q: What _____ do?

A: He _____
_____

4.

Q: What _____ do?

A: He _____ stop .
_____

5.

Q: How is he?

A: ....
....

6.

Q: What _____ do?

A: He _____
the living room.

D Think about two people in your native country. Answer the following questions about them in complete sentences on a separate piece of paper. Share your sentences with a partner.

1. What time is it in your native country? Where do you think the two people are right now? (use **must**)

2. What do you think those two people will possibly have for dinner tonight? (use **might**)

3. What is something they may not want to do next Sunday?

4. What do you think they should do for you on your next birthday?

5. Do they have to work?

A **"Must Be" Twenty Questions** One student will write down an occupation, show it only to the teacher, and stand in front of the class. The rest of the class will take turns asking twenty **yes-no** questions to try to figure out what the occupation is.

EXAMPLE:
Student 2: *Do you work outside?*
Student 1: *No, I don't.*
Student 3: *Is your job dangerous?*
Student 1: *No, it isn't.*
Student 4: *Do you help people?*
Student 1: *Yes, I do.*
Student 5: *Do you work in a hospital?*
Student 1: *Yes, I do.*
Student 6: *You **must be** a doctor!*
Student 1: *That's right! I'm a doctor.*

B **Role Play What's Wrong?**

Step 1: Your teacher will put your class in two teams, Team A and Team B. Each student will write on a slip of paper one kind of situation that can be a problem for people (feeling sick, being late, looking for something important, etc.).

Step 2: You'll fold your slips of paper so they can't be read and put them all into one bowl.

Step 3: One person from team A will take a slip of paper from the bowl and act out the situation in front of the class. Team A will have one minute to guess the situation and give advice using **should**.

The teams will take turns acting out the situations and guessing until all the slips of paper are gone. The team that guesses the most situations correctly wins.

C **Chant**

Hiring The Band

That must be the bandleader.
He's probably going to sing.
He must be married.
He's wearing a wedding ring.

Should I ask him for his number?
Should I ask him if he's free?
To play at our party?
Should I ask about his fee?

He might be the leader.
He must be in the band.
He could be the singer.
They're giving him a hand.

You should ask him for his schedule.
He might not be free
To play at your party in the afternoon at three.

He may be very happy to get your invitation.
He might be very pleased to have this conversation.
He might not be busy. He might be free.
But don't forget you have to ask about his fee.

Present Perfect Tense

Use the present perfect tense to talk about:

• actions or experiences in the past without knowing *exactly* when they happened.

Kevin's grandmother has had five jobs.

She has had many hobbies.

```
        ?       |
    past  present  future
```

• actions that began in the past and continue in the present.

Kevin's grandmother has been married for forty years.

She has lived in her house for twenty years.

```
    _____|_ _ _ _ _
    past  present  future
```

Present Perfect Form

Use **have** or **has** + the past participle of a verb.

The past participle of a regular verb is the same as its past tense form.

Base Form	Past Tense	Past Participle
learn	learned	learned

The past participle form of an irregular verb is usually different from its past tense form.

Base Form	Past Form	Past Participle
be	was/were	been
go	went	gone

Use these contractions with **have/has: I've, you've, we've, they've, he's, she's, it's**.

's can be part of a contraction with **BE** or **Has**.

Contraction with BE	Contraction with Has
She's married. = (She is ...)	She's been married twice. = (She has been...)

See Appendix A for a list of irregular verbs. See inside back cover for -ed spelling rules.

A Read about Kevin's active grandmother. Underline present perfect verbs (**have/has** + past participle). Then listen.

Kevin wants to learn more about his family, so he <u>has spent</u> some time interviewing his grandmother. His grandmother has had an interesting life. She has been married for 40 years. She has been a mother for 35 years. She has had five different jobs, and she has worked at her present job for the last ten years. She has been a waitress, a teacher, and the director of a school. She has lived in many houses during her life, and she and Kevin's grandfather have lived in this house for over 20 years. She has learned to ski, snowboard, and scuba dive. She has been an artist and a gardener, too.

B Write the past participles of the regular and irregular verbs in the box. Then complete the sentences in the present perfect tense. More than one answer is possible.

love	_loved_	learn	....	go	....
have	....	sleep	....	know	....
read	....	fly	....	try	....
see	....	visit	....	be	....

1. Grandma _has learned_ five languages.

2. Grandma .... her job for ten years.

3. Kevin and his sister .... in a small airplane with Grandma.

4. Grandma .... on a mountain in a tent.

5. Kevin and his sister .... many books about traveling.

6. Kevin and his sister .... many kinds of interesting food with Grandma.

7. Grandma .... around the world and .... lots of famous places.

8. Grandma .... and .... Grandpa for 42 years.

C Complete the chart with past forms and past participles. See Appendix A for the spelling of irregular verbs. Then test your partner on the past forms and past participles.

EXAMPLE: *(You) write   (Your Partner) wrote / written*

Base Form	Past	Past Participle
write	*wrote*	*written*
eat		
stop		
speak		
need		
get		
make		
carry		
do		
want		
take		

60

Present Perfect Tense with *Since* and *For*

Use the present perfect tense + **since** + a *specific point in time* to describe when a situation began. The situation started in the past and continues in the present.

Subject	Verb		Point in Time	
Denise	has owned	her salon	since 1995.	1995 2000 2005

Use a clause with **since** + subject + past tense verb to describe when a situation began. The situation started in the past and continues in the present.

	Subject	Verb		Subject	Verb	
Since	I	left	my country,	I	haven't had	a job.*
	I	haven't had	a job since	I	left	my country.

*When **since** is the first word in a sentence, add a comma.

Use the present perfect tense + **for** + time expression to describe the length of a situation that started in the past and continues in the present.

Subject	Verb		for + time expression	
Denise	has owned	her salon	for ten years.	1995 2000 2005
Alberto	hasn't had	a job	for six months.	

Language Notes:

• Some time expressions with **since**:
last week, last month, last year, 1999, last semester, since I came here

• Some time expressions with **for**:
ten years, five months, three days, one week, an hour, five minutes, several days, a few years, for a long time

• Contractions: he/she/it + has = he's, she's, it's
I/we/they + have = I've, we've, they've

A Alberto is applying for a job in a beauty salon. Listen to the conversation and draw a line from the circle with **for** or **since** to the time expressions you hear.

for

since

January
I left my country
ten years
twelve years
a long time
five months
many years
I came to this country

B Fill in the blanks with **for** or **since**.

Alberto has worked for Denise (1.) ~~for~~ six months, and he's learned a lot about her. Denise has been in the U.S (2.) _____ 20 years. She's lived in Boston (3.) _____ 1993. Denise loves working in her beauty salon. She's worked in the beauty business (4.) _____ over 20 years and she's owned her own salon (5.) _____ 1995. Denise and her husband haven't been back to Argentina (6.) _____ ten years and she hasn't seen her family (7.) _____ 1995. Denise and her husband hope to return for a visit soon. Their youngest child has finished high school and has been in college (8.) _____ a year and a half. Denise is happy to have Alberto working for her because she hasn't taken any days off work (9.) _____ March and she needs a break.

C Write five sentences about you and people you know. Choose people and time expressions from the lists below. Share your sentences with a partner. Then, on a separate piece of paper, write about your partner and people that he or she knows.

PEOPLE YOU KNOW	TIME EXPRESSIONS
your mother	for .... years
your parents	since (year)
your best friend	for a long time
you	since I finished high school
your classmate	since last week
your father	for five months
your sister or your brother	since last (month)
you and your family	for one hour

EXAMPLE: My parents have been in the U. S. for thirty years. They have been here since they got married.

1. _____
2. _____
3. _____
4. _____
5. _____

EXAMPLE *(about your partner):* Maria has had the same part-time job since she finished high school. She has been a college student for one year.

LESSON 61

Present Perfect Tense—Yes-No Questions with *Ever*, Statements with Frequency Adverbs and Expressions

Use **ever** in **Yes-No** questions in the present perfect tense to find out what experiences people have had.

Yes-No Questions	Short Answers	
Have you ever been in a hot air balloon?	Yes, I have.	No, I haven't.
Has he ever gone surfing?	Yes, he has.	No, he hasn't.

Use frequency adverbs with the present perfect tense to show *how often* you have done something.

I've never climbed a mountain.

I've hardly ever gone on a roller coaster because I'm too scared.

The frequency adverb comes between **have/had** and the past participle.

Use frequency words and expressions with the present perfect tense to show *how many times* you have done something.

I've gone mountain climbing a few times.

Frequency words and expressions: **once, twice, a couple of times, a few times, several times**

A Write the past participle of each verb in the box. Complete the questions with one of the past participles. Then listen and circle the correct answer to each question.

climb - *climbed*	take -	
jump -	be -	go - ....

1. Has Ted ever ....*been*........ on a roller coaster?

   Yes, he has.   No, he hasn't.

2. Has Ted ever .... surfing?

   Yes, he has.   No, he hasn't.

3. Has Ali ever .... a mountain?

   Yes, he has.   No, he hasn't.

4. Has Ali ever .... out of a plane?

   Yes, he has.   No, he hasn't.

5. Has Ted ever .... a hot air balloon ride?

   Yes, he has.   No, he hasn't.

B Write **yes-no** questions about Ted and Ali using the words in parentheses. Write answers in complete sentences. Use the present perfect tense.

1. (Ted/ever/travel alone)   Has Ted ever traveled alone?

   (yes/a few times) Yes. He's traveled alone a few times.

2. (Ali/ever/drive/to the mountains)

   (yes/often)

3. (Ted and Ali/ever/be/to L.A.)

   (yes/once)

4. (Ted/ever/go surfing)

   (no/never)

5. (Ali and Ted/ever/take a trip together)

   (yes/a couple of times)

6. (Ali/ever/get sick on a roller coaster)

   (yes/once)

C Chant

Life Experience

Have you ever fallen off a motorbike?
Have you ever gotten lost on a summer hike?
Have you ever gone swimming in the middle of the night?
Have you ever gotten angry and had a big fight?

> Well I've never fallen off a motorbike.
> I've never gotten lost on a summer hike.
> But I have gone swimming in the middle of the night.
> And I have gotten angry and had a big fight.

Have you ever sailed alone on the deep blue sea?
Have you ever put six lumps of sugar in your tea?
Have you ever heard the voice of a wild white dove?
Have you ever fallen madly, madly in love?

> No, I've never sailed alone on the deep blue sea.
> I've never put six lumps of sugar in my tea.
> I've never heard the voice of a wild white dove.
> But I have fallen madly, madly in love.

Review

Present Perfect Tense with *For*, *Since*, and *Ever*

A **Dictation** Karen is talking about love. Listen and write what you hear. Then underline the sentences in the present perfect tense. Circle the past participles. Put a box around **since** and **for**. Key words: *at first sight, immediately, guy, teenager*

Have you ever ....

....

....

....

....

....

....

B Look at the sentences below. Write **A** in the space on the left if the sentences go with diagram A; write **B** if they go with diagram B.

A We don't know when something happened in the past.

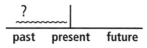

B Something started in the past and continues to the present.

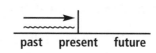

___A___ **1.** She has been divorced three times.

_____ **2.** She has known the guy for only two weeks.

_____ **3.** She has been this way since she was a teenager.

_____ **4.** My brother has tried to give her advice many times.

_____ **5.** I have told her to be careful more than once.

C On a separate piece of paper, rewrite part of the dictation from Exercise A. Write about twin cousins. Change **she** to **they, her** to **them**, and **guy** to **guys**.

FIRST SENTENCE: My twin cousins always fall in love immediately, but . . .

D Robert is a lottery winner. Read about his good luck and how it has changed his life. Then write a question for each of the answers below.

Believe it or not, I have won the lottery twice! And since I won all that money, my life has changed a lot. I have been on TV five times. I have given my family lots of presents and they have thanked me. But I haven't spent all the money only on myself. I have helped my community, too.

1. <u>Has Robert ever won the lottery</u>?

Yes, Robert has won the lottery twice.

2. ....?

Yes, his life has changed a lot.

3. ....?

No, his family hasn't been on TV.

4. ....?

Yes, he has given his family many presents.

5. ....?

No, he hasn't spent money only on himself.

6. ....?

Yes, he has helped his community.

E What does the contraction in each sentence mean? Write **is** or **has** on each line to the left.

<u>Has</u> **1.** She's fallen in love three times.

.... **2.** She's in love again!

.... **3.** He's given her a lot of advice.

.... **4.** He's a good brother.

.... **5.** It's an interesting story.

.... **6.** It's been an interesting year.

F Find the mistakes. Make the corrections.

Has
1. ~~Have~~ he met many people?

2. Since I have come to the U.S., I've met a lot of people.

3. We have been in school since two years.

4. They have had free time rarely.

5. She has spoken English with her children never.

6. They've never be on an airplane.

7. I have learn a lot.

8. Has he gone to the city ever?

G On a separate piece of paper, rewrite these sentences. Change **since** to **for** and **for** to **since**. Imagine that it is 2 p.m. and that today's date is Tuesday, August 18th, 2020.

EXAMPLE: *I have been in the U.S. since 2018. I have been in the U.S. for two years.*

1. He hasn't seen his family for a long time.

2. She has been on vacation since August 4th.

3. I haven't spoken English since Sunday!

4. We have been in this room for four hours.

5. They have had a lot of work for a week.

6. I've known her since 2012.

7. You've been absent for 10 days.

8. Since Sunday, it has been very cold.

Have Fun

A Crossword Puzzle: Past Participles

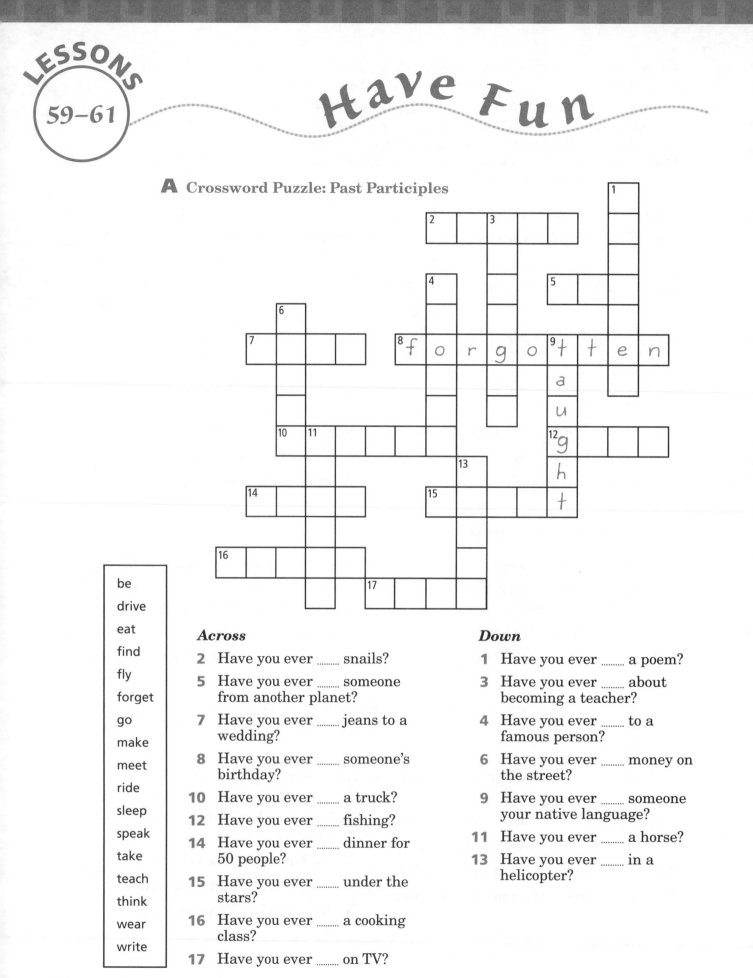

be
drive
eat
find
fly
forget
go
make
meet
ride
sleep
speak
take
teach
think
wear
write

Across

2 Have you ever .... snails?

5 Have you ever .... someone from another planet?

7 Have you ever .... jeans to a wedding?

8 Have you ever .... someone's birthday?

10 Have you ever .... a truck?

12 Have you ever .... fishing?

14 Have you ever .... dinner for 50 people?

15 Have you ever .... under the stars?

16 Have you ever .... a cooking class?

17 Have you ever .... on TV?

Down

1 Have you ever .... a poem?

3 Have you ever .... about becoming a teacher?

4 Have you ever .... to a famous person?

6 Have you ever .... money on the street?

9 Have you ever .... someone your native language?

11 Have you ever .... a horse?

13 Have you ever .... in a helicopter?

B Spelling Bee Stand in a line with your classmates. Your teacher will say the base form of a regular or irregular verb. One by one, students will spell the past participles of the verbs. When students make mistakes, they will sit down. The last student to spell a verb correctly is the winner.

C Chant

Dreaming About Peru

Have you ever been to Peru?
　　No, I haven't, have you?
I've been there a couple of times
To visit my old friend Sue.

　　Has Jill ever lived in Peru?
She's lived there since she was two.
Have you met her husband Kevin?
　　Yes, I met him in 1987.
Have you ever seen their son?
　　Yes, I saw him when he was one.
　　But I haven't seen him since then,
　　And I think today, he's ten.

　　You've been to Peru a couple of times.
　　So has my Aunt Marie.
　　Sometimes I think that everyone
　　Has been to Peru except me.

Present Perfect Tense—Statements and Questions with *Yet* and *Already*

Yet means **up to this moment** or **until now**.

STATEMENTS WITH *YET* and *ALREADY*

• Use **yet** in negative statements to show that an action was not completed.
I haven't joined any clubs yet, but I will.   The bus hasn't arrived yet.

• Use **already** in affirmative statements to show that an action has been completed.
I've already signed up for the International Students Club.

Language Notes:

• **Yet** comes at the end of questions and statements.

• **Already** comes between the helping verb and the main verb in a statement or at the end of a sentence.

QUESTIONS WITH *YET*:

• Ask **Yes-No** questions in the present perfect tense with **yet** to find out if an action was completed.*

Have you registered for classes yet?   Has class started yet?

* You can use **already** in a question to show surprise that an action was completed.

• Ask **Why** questions in the present perfect tense with **yet** to find out why an action has not been completed. Use the negative form.

Why haven't you registered yet?   Why hasn't class started yet?
Classes start tomorrow!   We've been waiting for ten minutes.

ANSWERS WITH *YET* and *ALREADY*

• Use **yet** in negative answers: No, I haven't registered for classes yet.

• Use **already** in affirmative answers: Yes, I have already registered for classes.

          OR: Yes, I have registered for classes already.

A Chang and Victor are starting a new semester at school. Listen to their conversation. Write checks in the chart to show what Victor has already done and what he hasn't done yet.

	Things Victor has already done	Things Victor hasn't done yet
registered for classes	✓	
bought his books		
joined the International Students Club		
called Eva		
told Eva about his new girlfriend		

B Write questions for the answers and answers to the questions. Use the present perfect tense and **yet, already,** or **why**.

1. (Victor/make/new friends)
   Q: Has Victor made new friends yet?
   A: Yes, he's already made several new friends.

2. (Victor/try/the new cafeteria)
   Q: ....
   A: No, he hasn't tried it yet.

3. (Why/Victor/[not]try/it)
   Q: ....
   A: Because he brings his lunch from home.

4.
   Q: Has Victor joined any clubs yet?
   (yes/he/join/two)
   A: ....

5. (Victor/be/to any parties)
   Q: ....
   A: Yes, he's already been to several parties.

6.
   Q: Has Victor had any exams yet?
   (no/have/any exams)
   A: ....

7. (Why/Victor/[not] have/any exams)
   Q: ....
   A: Because he has been in school for only one month.

8. (Victor/see Eva)
   Q: ....
   A: Yes, he's seen her a few times.

C Victor and Chang are now roommates, and they're having a party. Look at their to-do lists. On a separate piece of paper, write nine questions and answers about what they have already done and what they haven't done yet.

To Do-Victor	To Do-Victor and Chang	To Do-Chang
~~clean the bathroom~~	go shopping	~~wash the dishes~~
set the table	clean the house	put pizza in the oven
choose music	~~decorate the apartment~~	buy flowers

EXAMPLE: Q: Has Victor cleaned the bathroom yet?
          A: Yes, he's already cleaned the bathroom. OR
             Yes, he's cleaned the bathroom already.

LESSON 63

Present Perfect Tense—Questions with *How many times* and *How long*

> Ask a question in the present perfect tense with **How many times ...?** to find out the number of times someone has done something.
>
> Q: **How many times** have you seen a soccer game?
> A: Probably about four times./So many times, I can't count!/Never.
>
> $\begin{array}{ccc} x & x & x \mid \\ \text{past} & \text{present} & \text{future} \end{array}$
>
> Ask a question in the present perfect tense with **How long ...?** to find out the length of a situation.
>
> Answer **How long** questions with **for** or **since**.
>
> Q: **How long** have you been on a soccer team?
> A: **For** six years.　　　**OR**　　　A: **Since** 1999.
>
> $1999 \longrightarrow \mid$
> $\begin{array}{ccc} \text{past} & \text{present} & \text{future} \end{array}$
>
> (See Lesson 60 for more information on **for** and **since**.)

A Pedro and Kim are talking about playing and watching soccer. Listen to the conversation and fill in the chart below.

goalie

Soccer Experiences	How Long?	How Many Times?
has played on the school team (Kim)		
has played goalie (Kim)	for five years; since	
has won games (Kim)		
has traveled for a game this year (Kim)		
has been to games (Pedro)		
has played soccer (Pedro)		

B Kim wants to know about the sports Pedro plays. Underline the correct form in Kim's questions. Write the past participle of one of these verbs in each blank: be, go, play, run, see.

Kim's Questions	Pedro's Answers
1. (How long/How many times) have you ....played......... tennis?	For five years.
2. (How long/How many times) have you .... your favorite soccer team?	A few times.
3. (How long/How many times) have you .... interested in sports?	Since high school.
4. (How long/How many times) have you .... bowling?	Only a couple of times.
5. (How long/How many times) have you .... volleyball?	For three months.
6. (How long/How many times) have you .... in a marathon?	Many times. I love it.
7. (How long/How many times) have you .... a baseball player?	Since I was a kid.

C **Part 1** Ask a group of three students the questions in the left-hand column. Write the names of the students who say, "Yes." Then ask a question with **how long** or **how many times** and write the students' short answers.

Questions	Name(s)	How Long?	How Many Times?	Short Answer
Who plays tennis?				
Who has ever been on a roller coaster?				
Who has a job?				
Who has ever won a prize?				
Who plays soccer?				
Who has ever gone camping?				

Part 2 On a separate piece of paper, write six sentences about the students in your group. Use the information in the chart.

Contrast: Past vs. Present Perfect

Use the past tense to talk about something that happened at a *specific* time in the past.

Julia **found** a new job two weeks ago.

Tao's brother **called** him yesterday at 2:00 and at 7:30.

They **didn't have** English homework last night.

Use the present perfect tense to talk about something that:

• happened in the past, but we don't know/say exactly when.

Julia **has had** three job interviews.   They **have spoken** to each other a few times.

• started in the past and continues to the present.

Julia **has been** here for three years.

They **haven't seen** each other since August.

Time Expressions-Past		Time Expressions—Present Perfect
yesterday	for six months	for six months
last week/month/year	already	since 2001
a week ago/five years ago		ever (only in questions)
in 2001		yet/already

Language Note:

• Don't use a past time expression in a present perfect sentence.

Correct: Julia found a new job yesterday.   **Incorrect:** ~~Julia has found a new job yesterday.~~

See Appendix C for a list of time expressions.

A Read the story about Julia and Tao. Circle the verbs in the past tense and underline the verbs in the present perfect tense. Then listen.

Julia and Tao are new classmates. They (started) their English class three days ago. They've spoken to each other a few times and have learned many things about each other. Julia moved here three years ago from El Salvador with her family. She has attended several English classes and her English has improved. So, last month she decided to look for a job. She has had some job interviews and she hopes to find a job soon. Julia and her family have made many friends here.

Tao's experience has been very different. He arrived two months ago from China, and he came alone. His brother didn't come with him, and he's very sorry about that. He's made only one friend, so he's very lonely. Tao found a good apartment two weeks ago, and he has gotten some furniture. But he hasn't bought a TV yet. Julia has told him that things will get better soon and that he has to be patient.

B After class, Julia takes the bus home. She meets a former classmate on the bus. Read their conversation. Fill in each blank with a verb in the present perfect or past tense.

Natasha: Oh Julia, I'm so glad we have a few minutes to talk. (1. have)

...Have you had... any job interviews yet?

Julia: Uh-huh. I (2. have) .... three since I (3. see)

.... you at Andy's house. But I (4. [not] hear)

.... anything yet.

Natasha: I (5. have) .... a job interview yesterday. They (6.offer)

.... me the job right away, but I (7. [not]take)

.... it because it's too far away. I told them yesterday.

Julia: I'm sure you'll find something soon. (8. move) .... you

.... into your new apartment yet?

Natasha Uh-huh! I (9.move) .... in two weeks ago. I (10. meet)

.... a few of my neighbors already. And last weekend,

one of them (11. invite) .... me to dinner. I (12. have)

.... a great time.

Julia: That's great. Well, I have to go. Good luck with the interviews. I

know you'll get a good job!

C Chant

Good Movie

Have you seen any good movies lately?

I haven't seen a movie since July.

How about you?

I saw The Bow Wow Boys. I loved it.

So did I.

Didn't you love that performance by Johnny Jones?

I've seen every film he's made.

I saw one of his old movies last year:

Sitting Around in the Shade.

Oh, yeah, that was great. I saw that, too.

But The Bow Wow Boys is the movie for you.

Review

Present Perfect Tense with *Already, Yet, How many times, How long,* Past vs. Present Perfect Tenses

A **Dictation** A magazine reporter is talking to an elderly couple. Listen and write what you hear. Circle the *one* sentence that is in the past tense.
Key words: *happily, anniversary, great-grandchildren*

Interviewer:	*Thank you for letting me interview you.*
Mr. Wilson:	*No problem. We're always happy to give interviews.*
Interviewer:	....
Mrs. Wilson:	....
	....
Interviewer:	....
Mr. Wilson:	....
Interviewer:	....
Mrs. Wilson:	....
Interviewer:	....
Mrs. Wilson:	....
	....
Mr. Wilson:	....
Mrs. Wilson:	....
Interviewer:	....

B Look at the dictation and write a question for each answer.

1. *How long has Mrs. Wilson been married* ?

   Mrs. Wilson has been married since she was 22 years old.

2. ....?

   No, they haven't given the guest list to their great-granddaughter yet.

3. ....?

   Mr. and Mrs. Wilson haven't given her the list yet because they're not ready.

4. ....?

   They've given five or six interviews in the past ten years.

C Jackie Wilson is talking about her great-grandparents. Complete the sentences with the present perfect or past tense form of the verbs in parentheses. Circle the time expressions.

A few weeks ago, I (1. interview) ..... *interviewed* ..... my great-grandparents for many hours. I (2. ask) .... them a lot of questions about their travels, and I (3. learn) .... a lot. Last week, I (4. make) .... a DVD of our interview so our family will always have our history. I (5. already make) .... about 30 copies of the DVD to give as birthday presents to different members of our family.

When I interviewed my grandparents, they (6. tell) .... me that they (7. have) .... wonderful lives. They (8. know) .... each other since they (9. be) .... kids, and they (10. be) .... married for almost 80 years!

Their life together (11. be) .... very interesting. They (12. travel) .... all over the world and (13. meet) .... people from many different cultures. When they (14. be) .... in Italy in the summer of 1952, they (15. teach) .... English and (16. study) .... Italian. They (17. live) .... in India, China, Congo, and Brazil, too!

D Match numbers from column A and letters from column B to make complete sentences about Jackie and her husband. More than one answer may be possible, and you can use answers more than once. Write the letters for all possible answers on the lines. Imagine that the year is now 2020.

	A	**B**
c, g, h	**1.** Jackie has been a filmmaker	a. a few years ago.
....	**2.** She got interested in the career when she met her husband	b. for a few years.
....	**3.** They haven't made a film together	c. in 2014.
....	**4.** They talked about making a film together	d. a long time ago.
....	**5.** They met at work	e. yet.
....	**6.** They have been married	f. since 2016.
		g. since she graduated from college.

Have Fun

A **TV Talk Show Role Play** Get into groups of four. One student will be the TV host. The three other students will be guests on the show. The host will ask each guest questions about living in an English-speaking country. Perform your role play in groups or for the entire class. Be yourself or choose a role. Write your name and role on a folded piece of paper and put it on your desk.

Possible roles: *teacher, doctor, lawyer, computer programmer, parent of six children, psychologist, police officer, politician, actor, singer, etc.*

Hosts: Study the information on page 210.

B **Guessing Game** Write three true sentences and one false sentence about you. Write two sentences in the past tense and two sentences in the present perfect tense. Read your sentences to a small group or to your class. Your classmates will guess which sentence is false.

EXAMPLE:

You:	*I got married five years ago.*
	I was born in 1955.
	I have been to Canada.
	I haven't done my homework yet.
Your classmate:	*You weren't born in 1955. You're not that old!*
You:	*Yes, I am. I was born in 1955!*
Another classmate:	*You haven't been to Canada.*
You:	*That's right. I've never been there.*

C **Chant**

Music

How long have you studied music?
    I've studied since I was four.
How many lessons do you have in a week?
    I don't take lessons anymore.
How many hours a day do you practice?
    Usually three or four.
How often do you give a performance?
    I don't perform anymore.
Did you only study piano?
    No, I played the violin.
    My father played the piano.
    I used to play with him.
Have you ever played the cello?
    No, I haven't had the chance.
    But I've heard some wonderful cellists
    ever since I moved to France.

Appendices

Appendix A

Irregular Verbs

Base Form	Past Form	Past Particple	Base Form	Past Form	Past Particple
be	was/were	been	let	let	let
beat	beat	beaten	light	lit	lit
begin	began	begun	lose	lost	lost
bite	bit	bitten	make	made	made
break	broke	broken	mean	meant	meant
bring	brought	brought	meet	met	met
build	built	built	pay	paid	paid
buy	bought	bought	put	put	put
catch	caught	caught	quit	quit	quit
choose	chose	chosen	read	read	read
come	came	come	ride	rode	ridden
cost	cost	cost	ring	rang	rung
cut	cut	cut	run	ran	run
do	did	done	say	said	said
draw	drew	drawn	see	saw	seen
drink	drank	drunk	sell	sold	sold
drive	drove	driven	send	sent	sent
eat	ate	eaten	set	set	set
fall	fell	fallen	shake	shook	shaken
feed	fed	fed	show	showed	shown/showed
feel	felt	felt	sing	sang	sung
fight	fought	fought	sit	sat	sat
find	found	found	sleep	slept	slept
fly	flew	flown	speak	spoke	spoken
forget	forgot	forgotten	spend	spent	spent
freeze	froze	frozen	stand	stood	stood
get	got	gotten	steal	stole	stolen
give	gave	given	swim	swam	swum
go	went	gone	take	took	taken
grow	grew	grown	teach	taught	taught
hang	hung	hung	tear	tore	torn
have	had	had	tell	told	told
hear	heard	heard	think	thought	thought
hit	hit	hit	throw	threw	thrown
hold	held	held	understand	understood	understood
hurt	hurt	hurt	wake up	woke up	woken up
keep	kept	kept	wear	wore	worn
know	knew	known	win	won	won
leave	left	left	write	wrote	written

Appendix B

Irregular Verb Memorization Groups

Past form = past participle	**aught:** catch - caught - caught teach - taught - taught	**ent:** lend - lent - lent send - sent - sent spend - spent - spent	**aid:** say - said - said (like *bed*) pay - paid - paid (like *aid*)
	ought: bring - brought - brought buy - bought - bought fight - fought - fought think - thought - thought	**ept:** keep - kept - kept sleep - slept - slept	**old:** sell - sold - sold tell - told - told **stood:** stand - stood - stood understand-understood- understood
-en **Past participle**	**got - gotten:** get - got - gotten forget - forgot - forgotten	**oke - oken:** speak - spoke - spoken break - broke - broken wake - woke - woken	**(mixed)-en** (like *in*): beat - beat - beaten choose - chose - chosen drive - drove - driven eat - ate - eaten fall - fell - fallen give - gave - given hide - hid - hidden ride - rode - ridden steal - stole - stolen take - took - taken write - wrote - written
Other	**ew - own:** blow - blew - blown fly - flew - flown grow - grew - grown know - knew - known throw - threw - thrown BUT: draw - drew - drawn show - showed - shown	**ang - ung:** ring - rang - rung sing - sang - sung	**No change:** cost - cost - cost cut- cut - cut fit - fit - fit hit - hit - hit hurt - hurt - hurt let - let - let put - put - put quit - quit - quit read - read - read (like *red*) set - set - set

Appendix C

Time Expressions

Present Tense	Present Continuous Tense	Future Tense
every	now	today
minute	right now	tomorrow
morning	at this moment	the day after tomorrow
day	these days	two weeks from tomorrow
Saturday		
week		*in*
month	**Present Continuous Tense to show near-future meaning**	an hour
fall		two weeks
year		2050
	today	
on	tomorrow	*next*
Sunday(s)	at noon	week
Monday(s)	at 6:00	month
weekday(s)	next week	year
weekend(s)		
	in	*at*
Frequency Adverbs:	a few minutes	noon
always	five minutes	midnight
almost always	an hour	6:00
usually		
often	*this*	*on*
sometimes	morning	Sunday
rarely	afternoon	Monday
hardly ever	evening	
never	Saturday	*this*
	week	morning
	month	afternoon
Other Expressions:	fall	evening
once in a while	year	Saturday
in general		week
as a rule		month
		fall
once a week		year
twice a week		
three times a month		

continued on page 201

Time Expressions

Past Tense	Past Continuous Tense	Present Perfect Tense

yesterday
   morning
   afternoon
   evening
 	
   the day before yesterday
	yesterday
	Tuesday
	last month
	last year
	
	while I was } studying. . .
		for
		   five minutes
		   two days
		   one month
		   six years
		   a long time

last
   night
   week
   month
   year
   spring
		since
		   yesterday
		   last night
		   Tuesday
		   2002
		   May

in
   1950
   the 20th century
		Frequency Adverbs:
		   always
		   almost always
		   usually
		   often
		   sometimes
		   rarely
		   hardly ever
		   never

at
   noon
   midnight
   6:00		

for three years		

ago
   an hour ago
   a year ago
   two years ago		

when
   I was 16
   you arrived
   she was in school		

Appendix D

Infinitives and Their Families

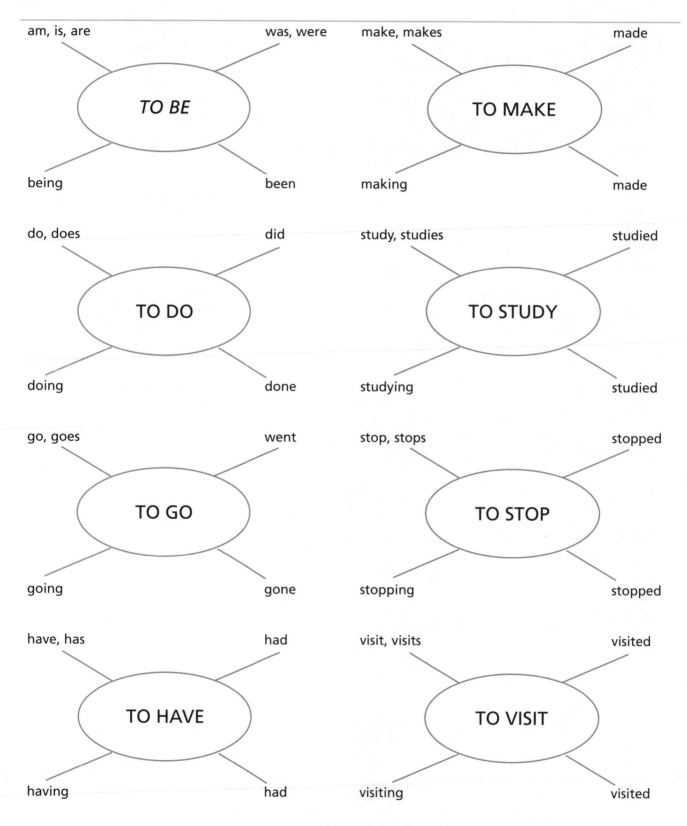

am, is, are   was, were

TO BE

being   been

make, makes   made

TO MAKE

making   made

do, does   did

TO DO

doing   done

study, studies   studied

TO STUDY

studying   studied

go, goes   went

TO GO

going   gone

stop, stops   stopped

TO STOP

stopping   stopped

have, has   had

TO HAVE

having   had

visit, visits   visited

TO VISIT

visiting   visited

Appendix E

Non-Action Verbs

Senses	Feelings	Opinion	Possession	Mental States	Other
feel	feel	agree	belong	forget	be
hear	hate	believe	have	know	cost
look	like	disagree	own	remember	mean
see	love	feel		understand	need
smell		think			owe
sound					want
taste					

Appendix F

Pronouns and Possessive Adjectives

Subject Pronouns	Object Pronouns	Possessive Adjectives	Possessive Pronouns	Reflexive Pronouns
I	me	my	mine	myself
you (singular)	you	your	yours	yourself
he	him	his	his	himself
she	her	her	hers	herself
it	it	its	----	itself
we	us	our	ours	ourselves
you (plural)	you	your	yours	yourselves
they	them	their	theirs	themselves

Appendix G

Comparative and Superlative Spelling

	Adjectives	Comparative Adjectives	Superlative Adjectives
1-syllable adjectives:	fast	faster (than)	the fastest
	large	larger (than)	the largest
	big	bigger (than)	the biggest
2-syllable adjectives that end in *y*:	funny	funnier (than)	the funniest
Adjectives that have two or more syllables and don't end in *y*:	beautiful	more beautiful (than)	the most beautiful
Irregular forms:	good	better (than)	the best
	bad	worse (than)	the worst
	far	farther (than)	the farthest
	a little	less (than)	the least

Appendix H

Prepositions of Time and Place

TIME

in	on	at	from . . . to . . .
A month: in April	**A day:** on Monday on New Year's Day on Saturday morning on Sunday night	**A time:** at 3:00 p.m. at 1 o'clock at noon at midnight	**from ___ to ___:** from 9:00 to 11:00 from Saturday to Sunday from 2005 to 2006
A year: in 2006	**A date:** on January 1st on the 4th of July on March 28th, 1978		
A season: in the summer	**A/the weekend:** on a weekend in July on the weekend on weekends		
Parts of a day: in the morning in the afternoon in the evening		**Part of a day:** at night	
The future: in ten minutes in two years			

PLACE

in	on	at	from . . . to . . .
A city/a state/ **a country/the world:** in London in Florida in Canada in the world	**Surfaces:** on the first floor on the wall on the ceiling on (the) earth	**Places:** at home at work at school at the supermarket at the post office	**from ___ to ___:** from Los Angeles to Mexico City
Transportation: in a car in a taxi	**Transportation:** on a bus on a plane on a train on a boat		
A room: in the kitchen	**A street:** on Fifth Avenue	**An address:** at 1600 Fifth Avenue	
Some places outside: in the park in the garden in the yard			

Appendix I

Phrases with Prepositions

Common Verb and Preposition Combinations

adjust **to** a new school
agree **with** an idea
apologize **for** doing something wrong
apply **for** a job
apply **to** a university
believe **in** fighting for an idea
borrow money **from** a friend
care **about** learning
compare this **to** that
complain **about** the bad weather
concentrate **on** doing a good job
depend **on** a friend
dream **about** going on vacation
forget **about** an appointment
hear **about** the news
help **with** moving to a new house
lend money **to** my sister

listen **to** music
look **at** a picture
look **for** his keys
look forward **to** going home
participate **in** a group
protect someone **from** danger
provide someone **with** help
stare **at** a picture
succeed **in** learning
take advantage **of** an opportunity
take care **of** a baby
talk **about** getting a new job
talk **to** your doctor
thank him **for** the present
think **about** studying medicine
vote **for** a candidate
wait **for** me

Common Adjective and Preposition Combinations

be...
absent **from** class
afraid **of** dogs
aware **of** danger
bored **with** her job
capable **of** getting good grades
concerned **about** safety
different **from** your brother
disappointed **in** the movie
divorced **from** each other
done with **your** homework
engaged **to** each other
excited **about** going away
familiar **with** him
famous **for** being a good dancer
finished **with** their homework
good **at** soccer
guilty **of** murder

interested **in** learning English
late **for** work
married **to** each other
nervous **about** flying
perfect **for** you
prepared **for** a test
proud **of** them
related **to** each other
responsible **for** your family
sad **about** leaving
satisfied **with** your work
successful **in** everything you do
sure **about** quitting your job
surprised **at** you
tired **of** working
upset **about** forgetting an appointment
worried **about** being on time

Appendix J

Modals and Have to

Modals/Meanings	Affirmative	Negative	Yes-No Questions
can-ability (present and future)	She can drive.	She can't drive.	Can she drive?
could-ability (past)	When he was ten, he could run very fast.	When he was ten, he couldn't vote.	Could he run very fast when he was ten?
could-possibility	They could be at the movies.	They couldn't be at the movies.	Could they be at the movies?
may-possibility	We may stay out late.	We may not get home early.	- - - -
might-possibility	She might know how to help us.	She might not know how to do it.	- - - -
must (making logical conclusions)	Their car is here, so they must be home.	Their car isn't here, so they must not be home.	- - - -
must-necessity	You must do your homework. (**Have to** is more common.)	- - - -	- - - -
have to-necessity	•I have to do my homework. •I had to do my homework before I went to work.	•I don't have to do my homework now. I can relax. •I didn't have to do homework when I was in first grade.	•Do I have to do my homework now? •Did you have to do homework when you were very young?
will-future •100% sure •offer •refuse •promise	•I will see you tomorrow. •I'll help you. - - - - •I promise I'll be there.	I won't see you tomorrow. - - - - •I won't go. •I promise I won't smoke.	Will I see you tomorrow? - - - - - - - - - - - -
should-advice	•You should relax. •You should come to class early tomorrow.	•You shouldn't be here right now. •You shouldn't come to class tomorrow.	•Should we go there now? •Should we go there tomorrow?

Appendix K

Adjectives + Infinitives (I'm afraid to go. / It is easy to drive.)

BE

afraid	expensive	happy	lucky
difficult	fun	hard	ready
easy	glad	important	sad

Appendix L

Common Non-Count Nouns

Collection of very small things	Liquid or semi-solid	Abstractions (things we can't touch) & categories / groups of things	
dirt	butter	advice	jewelry
dust	cheese	baggage	knowledge
flour	coffee	behavior	luck
fur	cream	clothing	luggage
grass	gasoline	crime	mail
hair	ice	education	money
pepper	lotion	equipment	music
rice	milk	food	news
salt	oil	freedom	permission
sand	soap	friendship	progress
sugar	soup	fun	scenery
	tea	furniture	time
	toothpaste	happiness	traffic
	water	hardware	underwear
		help	violence
		homework	weather
		information	work

Appendix M

Special Nouns

Irregular Plural		Always Plural	
child – children	person – people	clothes	pants
foot – feet	tooth – teeth	glasses	scissors
man – men	woman – women	jeans	shorts
mouse - mice		pajamas	

Communication Gap Instructions for Student A

Have Fun Lessons 14–17, page 54

STEP 1 Student A: Write the questions. Do not write short answers now.

Questions	Short Answers
1. What/doing/they/this afternoon/are	
2. What/tonight/doing/they/are	
3. What time/start/the show/does	
4. What/they/are/the 21st/do/going to/on	
5. What/Suzanne's birthday/on/do/they/going to/are	
6. When/Spanish class/Suzanne's /does/start	

STEP 2 Student A: Student B will ask you questions about Suzanne and Larry's plans. Answer the questions with information from this calendar. Use **will probably** to talk about uncertain plans. A question mark (?) on the calendar means the plans are not certain. (Talk, don't write.)

APRIL

Sunday	Monday	Tuesday	Wednesday	Thursday	Friday	Saturday
2 TODAY	3	4	5	6 Nick-4 pm doctor	7	8
9	10	11	12	13	14 mail taxes	15 Suzanne's birthday!!!
16 Larry-Portland Flight 260 Leave 9:00 am / Arrive 11:15 am	17 Anniversary- dinner out?	18	19	20	21	22

STEP 3 Student A: Ask Student B the questions at the top of this page. Write short answers on the lines to the right.

Communication Gap Instructions for Student A

Have Fun Lessons 18–20, page 65

Exercise B

STEP 1 **Student A:** Stay on this page and don't look at page 65. Ask Student B **yes-no** and **Wh** questions about George and Paul's cleaning schedule. Use the information to complete the calendar.

	Monday	Tuesday	Wednesday	Thursday	Friday	Saturday	Sunday
George	---------	dishes	---------	---------	---------	---------	nothing
Paul	laundry	---------	take out garbage	dishes	shopping	wash the car	---------

EXAMPLE QUESTIONS: *Does George do his laundry on Fridays?*
What does George do on Fridays?

STEP 2 **Student A:** Student B will ask you **yes-no** and **Wh** questions about George and Paul's cleaning schedule. Answer the questions using information from the calendar in Step 1.

TV Talk Show Role Play Instructions for Host

Have Fun Lessons 62–64, page 196

Exercise A

Possible ways to start your TV show:

Welcome to the *Good Afternoon Show*! Let's meet our guests. On the left we have ....,
in the middle we have ...., and on the right we have ....
Today I'm going to ask each of you some questions about your life in this country.
OK, my first question is for ....?

Possible interview questions:

(What you ask will really depend on what happens during your interviews.)

- How long have you been here?   OR   When did you come here?
- Why did you come?
- Have you had a good life here?
- Have you had any trouble with English? (If "Yes") What was the problem?
- Have you ever been sorry about coming?
  (If "Yes") Why were you sorry?   OR   (If "No") Why haven't you been sorry?
- Have you ever gone back to your native country?
  (If "Yes") How many times have you gone back?
- How long have you been: a singer? retired?
- What goals did you have when you came here? Have you reached your goals yet?

Possible responses to what your guests say:

That's interesting./I'm happy to hear that./I'm sorry to hear that./That's great!/
That's terrible./Really? That's amazing!

Possible way to end your interview:

Well, thank you all very much. It's been a pleasure talking to you, and we've learned a lot about
your lives and experiences over the years. We'll be right back after this . . .

Listening Script

Lesson 4

A

Babysitter
We need a babysitter to pick up our daughter from school. We want someone who has a car and drives carefully.
Call Linda at 555-2054.

Receptionist
We need someone who speaks English well. Many of our customers are from other countries, so we want someone who can speak slowly and clearly.
Call Peter at 555-3752.

Secretary
We need someone who can speak English fluently. We want a fast worker who can work well with other people. We want someone who types fast—at least 70 words per minute.
Call Mike at 555-2303.

Lesson 5

A

Anna: Joe! Where are you? I'm so worried about you. I heard the news about the accident on the radio.
Joe: I'm fine, but the traffic isn't moving.
Anna: I heard that a truck went through the tunnel in the wrong direction and hit a lot of cars.
Joe: That's right. I was driving over the bridge when the accident happened.
Anna: I'm glad you're OK. Listen, we have a meeting with Amy's teacher at 7 o'clock.
Joe: I know. Can you go to the meeting without me?
Anna: OK, but maybe you can come later. It's in room . . .

Joe: Wait. I need to find a piece of paper. OK. Go ahead.
Anna: It's in Room 252. It's on the second floor of Building E.
Joe: And what's the name of Amy's teacher? I forgot!

Review of lessons 1–5

A

Melissa works with children at a school in New York. She arrives early and spends six hours a day with the kids. She teaches them numbers and the letters of the alphabet. When the children are tired, she reads them stories. They sit quietly and listen. When the children don't behave well, Melissa talks to them. When it is necessary, she calls their parents. Her job as a teacher can be hard, but she's very happy.

Lesson 7

A

Dear Annie,
  I have a problem. I have two boyfriends, Mark and John. Mark is handsome, but he isn't very nice to me. For example, last week I got angry at him because he didn't remember my birthday.
  My other boyfriend is John. He isn't very handsome, but he is very kind to me. Last week he called me, took me to an expensive restaurant, and sent me flowers. I like him a lot, but I'm really in love with Mark.
  Last week both Mark and John invited me to the senior dance. Should I go with Mark or John?
  Confused

Lesson 8

A

Interviewer: So Mylo, tell me about your childhood. Were you born in Mexico City?
Mylo: No, I wasn't. I was born in a small village.
Interviewer: Were you interested in music as a child?
Mylo: Yes. I started to play the guitar when I was eight.
Interviewer: Wow! That's young! Tell me about your life now.
Mylo: Well, I'm married now. My wife and I have a daughter. She'll be two next week.
Interviewer: Congratulations! And what are your future plans?
Mylo: Well, I'll be in Europe next month.
Interviewer: Will you be in Miami again soon?
Mylo: No, I'm sorry I won't.
Interviewer: That's too bad for us. Well, good luck on your tour!

Lesson 9

A

Here is a typical evening at my house. My son Mark takes the bus home from school. His bus usually arrives at the bus stop at 5:00 p.m. After I pick him up at the bus stop, we go home and I cook dinner. Then my son goes to his room, plays computer games, and emails his friends. When my husband Charlie comes home, he has a snack and relaxes on the couch. After we eat dinner, my husband washes the dishes and I sometimes watch TV.
  My son never wants to do his homework. I always have to shout, "Do your homework!" He usually does his homework before he goes to bed.

Review of 6–9

A

Mike doesn't want to go to the doctor every year for a check-up, but he goes. Before he goes, he gets very nervous because he worries about his health. When he is in the doctor's office, he answers many questions. But he doesn't like the doctor's questions about exercise. Mike likes to sit on the couch, relax, eat junk food, and watch TV. He's a couch potato.

Lesson 10

A

Lynn: Hi, Janet. What are you doing right now?
Janet: Well, I'm trying to write my essay, but I can't concentrate. My neighbor is playing loud music. Can you hear it?
Lynn: Yes! That's terrible. Does he always make so much noise?
Janet: Yes. He plays in a band once a week. He and his friends practice every night, and I'm getting tired of it. So, what are you doing now? Do you want to meet me at Biff's Café?
Lynn: Sure!

Lesson 11

A

Dear Mom,
Hi! I hope all is well. School is OK. As you know, I'm taking three classes: English, art, and math. I like the art and English classes, but I'm having trouble with my math class. The teacher knows that the class is difficult for me. She often helps me with my homework after class, but I still don't understand it. In fact, I'm thinking about dropping my math class.
Mom, please understand. I have a lot of homework in my other classes. I want to get good grades at school, so I really think that I should drop the class. Please don't be angry!
Love, Paula

Lesson 13

A

Sylvia: I need to get some cash. Let's stop at the ATM. You know Bob, when I was young, we didn't have ATMs. We used to wait in line at the bank to withdraw money.
Bob: Really?
Sylvia: Yes. I remember that I used to go to the bank during my lunch hour. Sometimes I didn't have time for lunch!
Bob: So, do you think things are easier now, Grandma?
Sylvia: Well, I think in many ways, life used to be easier. For example, when I was a child, we never used to buy milk in the grocery store. The milkman used to deliver milk to our house. And when we were sick, the doctor used to come to our house, too. We didn't have to drive to the doctor's office.
Bob: Wow! Did you used to ride a horse to school, too?
Sylvia: Come on, Bob! I'm not *that* old!

Review of 10–13

A

I used to dream about being on TV, and last year I got free tickets to a TV show in Hollywood. I took my best friend with me, and we arrived early to get good seats. But we didn't get in right away. We stood in line for about an hour, and then we finally went in. After a while, the director talked to the audience and showed us the "applause" signs. I thought that was funny. After that, the star of the show came out and joked with us. Then we had to be very quiet, and the show started. When the applause signs went on, we made a lot of noise. The show wasn't very interesting, but we had a good experience.

Lesson 14

A

Anne: Your brother called this morning. Are you going to call him back?
Charlie: No, I'm not going to call him. I'm too busy.
Anne: But it's his birthday tomorrow.
Charlie Oh, you're right!
Anne: Are you going to buy him a present?
Charlie: Maybe . . . I think I'm going to get him a fishing rod. He and Nancy are going to retire soon, and I know they both enjoy fishing.
Anne: That's true. You know, we should invite them over for dinner Saturday.
Charlie: Good idea!
Anne: Wait! I forgot. We're not going to be home.
Charlie: Why not?
Anne: Remember? It's our anniversary. You're going to take me out to dinner!

Lesson 15

A

1. Theresa: Please come to the wedding.
   Emily: I promise I'll be there.
2. Theresa: They're getting married, and they're only twenty.
   Emily: They love each other very much. I'm sure they'll be happy.
3. Theresa: I have so much to do.
   Emily: I'll help you. Call any time.
4. Theresa: We're going to meet his parents tomorrow for lunch.
   Emily: I hope you'll like each other.

5. Theresa: Please don't tell them that I'm worried.
   Emily: Don't worry. I won't.
6. Theresa: There are so many invitations to write.
   Emily: I'll write them for you.
7. Emily: Are you planning to order flowers?
   Theresa: Yes, I think I'll buy roses.
8. Emily: Let me do the invitations for you!
   Theresa: No, I won't let you! It's too much work.
9. Emily: Are they going to go on a honeymoon?
   Theresa: No, they probably won't. They don't have much money.
10. Emily: I don't have a car.
    Theresa: I'll find someone to give you a ride.
11. Emily: Be happy for them! Try to relax!
    Theresa: OK, I'll try.

Lesson 17

A

Mrs. Cho: Hello, Mr. Parker. Nice to see you!
Mr. Parker: Hi, Mrs. Cho. Look at all the beautiful flowers you're buying!
Mrs. Cho: I need lots of flowers today! It's a very special occasion.
Mr. Parker: Is your son Steve graduating today?
Mrs. Cho: Yes, he is. We're all so proud of him.
Mr. Parker: Congratulations! Is he going to college right away?
Mrs. Cho: No, he's not. He's going to help my husband in the hardware store for a year or two.
Mr. Parker: That's wonderful! So when is his graduation?
Mrs. Cho: Well, it begins at 2:00 this afternoon. And then, right after the ceremony, we're having a big party. Would you like to join us? Lots of people are coming.
Mr. Parker: Thanks for the invitation, but I need to stay here at the store until it closes.

Mrs. Cho: What time does it close?
Mr. Parker: At 5:00.
Mrs. Cho: Well, how about coming by tomorrow? Steve would love to see you.
Mr. Parker: I'm sorry. We're flying to Chicago tomorrow morning for a family visit. Our flight leaves at 7:00.
Mrs. Cho: That's so early! How are you getting to the airport?
Mr. Parker: We're taking a cab.
Mrs. Cho: Well, I hope you have a wonderful time. I've got to run. Bye!

Review 14–17

A

Art and I leave at 6:00 tomorrow morning for Seattle. Before we leave, I'm going to drink a cup of strong coffee. We're driving separately. If we get there by lunchtime, I'll be happy. When we get there, we're going to unload the truck, and Art will return it right away. I'll follow him to the truck rental place, and then we'll take a break and have lunch. If we don't rest for a little while, we'll be exhausted. After we have lunch, we'll start unpacking. I hope we'll be OK. Moving is so much work!

Lesson 18

A

Marta: Did you come to this country by yourself?
Anya: No, I came here with some other students.
Miles: Were you born in a small town?
Anya: No, I wasn't. I was born in a big city.
Tom: Are you having a good time at this school?
Anya: Yes, I'm having a wonderful time.
Marta: Do you think American boys are cute?
Anya: Of course I do!

Miles: Are you ready to go back to your country?
Anya: Not at all!
Tom: Does your family miss you?
Anya: Of course. I miss my family, too!
Marta: Are you leaving soon?
Anya: Uh-huh. I'm leaving in about four weeks.
Miles: Will you come back to visit us?
Anya: I hope so!

Lesson 19

A

Hi. I'm Pam, and I'd like to tell you about my grandfather Marvin. He was born in Europe in a small town. He and his family came to the United States when he was still a young child. They came to the United States by boat because there were no airplanes then. He told me that it was a long, terrible trip and everyone got very sick on the boat.

My grandfather worked very hard all his life. Now he's retired and living in Florida. He's not working anymore, and he loves to play cards with his friends. There is a special clubhouse near his house, and every day he and his friends meet at the clubhouse to play cards.

I live far away from my grandfather, so I don't see him very much. I'm going to see him next week because my boss is sending me to Florida to do a project. I'm so excited. I'll have a chance to see my grandfather!

Lesson 20

A

Mom: How are you doing?
John: I'm doing fine.
Mom: How's your roommate Paul?
John: He's OK, but he's not a very neat person. He doesn't do anything around the house.

Mom: What do you mean?
John: Well, he likes to cook, but after he eats, he never does the dishes. And he never does his laundry. His dirty clothes are in a big pile next to his bed.
Mom: Oh, my! Do you tell him to clean up?
John: Yes, I asked him to wash the dishes last night, but he didn't do them. He just left the dishes in the sink.
Mom: That's terrible. Do you wash your dishes, John?
John: Of course, mom. I always clean up!
Mom: Well, tell Paul that he has to do something around the house. Tell him if he doesn't do any chores, you'll look for a new roommate. By the way, how's school? Do you have a lot of homework?
John: Yes. In fact, I'm doing my homework right now.

Review 18–20

A

Reporter: Ms. Bates, what are your plans to improve our schools?
Ms. Bates: I'm going to do a lot. I will do my best to give our children everything they need.
Reporter: What did you do for education when you were a mayor?
Ms. Bates: I did a lot of work. I started programs for parents. I did my best to help our kids learn.
Reporter: Did you help teachers?
Ms. Bates: I sure did.
Reporter: Were you successful?
Ms. Bates: Yes, in some ways. But I will do more when I'm governor.
Reporter: Where are you going to get the money?
Ms. Bates: Don't worry. I'll find it.
Reporter: Were you careful with money when you were a mayor?
Ms. Bates: I sure was! Why are you asking me that question? I did a great job as mayor!

Lesson 21

A

Dan: So, how was the party, Nina?
Nina: Great!
Dan: Who did you go with?
Nina: I went with a lot of kids from school.
Dan: Who drove you home?
Nina: Cindy. She has her driver license.
Dan: Who was at the party?
Nina: Lots of people. Hey—listen to this news. Jan's getting married!
Dan: What! Who's getting married?
Nina: Jan.
Dan: But she's so young! Who's she going to marry?
Nina: I don't know. A guy she works with.
Dan: Why is she getting married so young?
Nina: Who knows? Maybe she's really in love. I think she'll be very happy. Anyway, I met a very nice guy at the party.
Dan: Really? Who is he?
Nina: I'll tell you later. Oh, I need to make a call. Who has my cell phone?
Dan: I have it. Who do you want to talk to now?

Lesson 22

A

A: Bye, John. I'll see you Monday.
B: Bye, Julie. Uh . . .Wait! Do you need a ride home?
A No, thanks. I have my car.
B: Where do you live?
A: In Maplewood.
B: Maplewood? That's really far from here! Do you always drive to school?
A: Uh-huh.
B: How long does it take you to get here?
A: Well, it depends on the traffic. Sometimes it takes about an hour and a half.

B: Wow!
A: But I only come to school on Mondays, Wednesdays and Fridays, so it's not so bad.
B: Well, be careful on the road. Have a good weekend!
A: You too!

A: Excuse me. I'm looking for the art museum. Do you know how to get there?
B: Are you walking or driving?
A: I'm walking. How far is it from here?
B: Uh, I think about two miles. You can take the bus. It stops right at this corner.
A: How often does the bus come?
B: About every five minutes.
A: And how long does it take to get there by bus?
B: Well, the bus makes a lot of stops. It probably takes about ten minutes.
A: Thanks!

Lesson 23

A

Nick: Laura! It's time to go to school. Aren't you getting up? Doesn't school start at 8:30?
Laura: I don't have to get up early. I'm not going to school today.
Nick: Why aren't you going?
Laura: Didn't I tell you? We don't have school today
Nick: Oh right, I forgot! So, what are you going to do?
Laura: I'm going to the movies with my friend Sam.
Nick: But don't you have homework to do?
Laura: Yes, we both have homework, but we can do it when we get home.
Nick: Why don't you stay home and do your homework together?
Laura: Don't worry, Dad. We don't have much. We can do it tonight.

Lesson 24

A

1. The Olympic games began in Greece more than 2,000 years ago, but the modern Olympics didn't begin until 1898.
2. Many countries didn't send athletes to the first modern Olympics.
3. There weren't many sports at the first modern Olympics, but today, there are hundreds of sports.
4. Not every sport is played in the Olympics. For example, windsurfing is an Olympic sport, but skateboarding and golf aren't.
5. A long time ago, women didn't participate in the Olympics.
6. Some countries still don't send women athletes to the Olympics.
7. Now soccer is popular in the U.S., but it wasn't popular 30 years ago.
8. The U.S. has many good Olympic teams, but it didn't always have the best teams.
9. The 2012 Olympics won't be in New York. They might be in Paris.
10. Some people think that Olympic medal winners shouldn't be able to make a lot of money in advertisements.

Review 21–24

A

Brad Jr.: Dad, can I take the car to Adam's house?
Brad Sr.: Who's Adam?
Brad Jr.: He's a kid in my class.
Brad Sr.: Oh, right. Weren't you at his house last Saturday?
Brad Jr.: Uh-huh.
Brad Sr.: Who else is going to be there?
Brad Jr.: I don't know. Probably his parents.
Brad Sr.: Oh, don't I know them? Aren't they doctors?

Brad Jr.: I don't think so. I think they're lawyers.
Brad Sr.: Well, how far is Adam's house from here?
Brad Jr.: About ten minutes, I think.
Brad Sr.: How long will you be there?
Brad Jr.: I'm not sure. Maybe a couple of hours.
Brad Sr.: Don't you have to clean your room?
Brad Jr.: It isn't dirty.
Brad Sr.: Can't you ride your bike?
Brad Jr.: No, I can't. I have a flat tire.
Brad Sr.: Well, why don't we fix it?
Brad Jr.: Dad, *please* let me drive!

Lesson 25

A

Mom: What a mess! Please help us clean up, Mollie.
Mollie: OK, Mom. Whose umbrella is this?
Dad: That's ours. Just put it in the closet.
Mollie: OK. And what about this hat?
Mom: Oh. That's my sister's hat. I'll take it to her house tomorrow.
Mollie: And how about these gloves?
Dad: I think they're Grandma's gloves.
Mom: Let me see them. No, they're not hers. They're men's gloves. In fact, they're yours.
Dad: Are you sure they're mine? I've never seen them before.
Mom: I'm positive. I bought them for you last year.
Dad: How did they end up in the living room?

Lesson 26

A

Sonia: Hey, Marta, I love your earrings. Where did you get them?
Marta: My boyfriend bought them for me. I wear them every day.

Sonia: I didn't know that you had a new boyfriend!
Marta: Well, I do. His name is Victor. I met him two months ago.
Sonia: Well, the earrings look great on you. Victor has good taste.
Marta: Thanks. I agree. Let me see your purse. Wow! Is it new?
Sonia: Uh huh. I bought it on sale at the mall last week. I love it.
Marta: It's really beautiful. So, what are you doing these days?
Sonia: Well, my brother and I are taking a grammar class at the college. Grammar isn't easy for us.
Marta: Is the class fun?
Sonia: It's difficult, but we're enjoying it very much.

Lesson 28

A

Linda: Did you like the restaurant?
Bob: Yes, I did. Everything was delicious. But I'm a little disappointed. No one called me today to say, "Happy Birthday."
Linda: You're right. I'm sorry, Bob. Hey, look! We're passing Uncle Dan's house. Let's stop and say, "hello."
Bob: I don't think anyone is home. Hello! Is anyone there? I hear something. I think someone is coming.
Uncle Dan: Hi, Bob! Hi, Linda. I'm sorry it took me so long to answer the door.
Bob: Uncle Dan, why is it so dark in here? Is anything wrong?
Uncle Dan: No, nothing is wrong. Come on in.
Bob's friends: Surprise! Happy birthday, Bob!
Bob: Wow! Everyone is here!

Review 25–28

A

Nobody understands how I feel. My mother-in-law thinks my kitchen is her kitchen. But it's mine and not hers! When she comes over, she makes herself at home. Then she tells me she wants to cook with me. But I want to cook by myself! I know she thinks I can't cook anything well. Everyone else, especially my husband, likes my cooking. I think she still wants to take care of her son.

Lesson 29

A

Ted: Let's take a walk.
Kay: OK, but it's going to get dark soon. We need our flashlights.
Ted: Flashlights! Oh, no! I can't believe it! I forgot the flashlights.
Kay: Well, I guess we can't take a walk. Let's just stay here. Where are our jackets? It's getting cold.
Ted: Uh-oh. Didn't you pack them?
Kay: No. I thought *you* did! Well, I guess I'll go and wash my face, brush my teeth, and get into my sleeping bag . . . Here's a towel and there's the soap. We have three toothbrushes here, but I don't see the toothpaste. I forgot to pack it! And Jenny's medicine isn't in here!
Ted: Boy, I don't think we're very organized. I sure hope Jenny brought her homework. Jenny—where are you?
Jenny: Over here, Dad.
Ted: Did you remember to bring your homework?
Jenny: Oh no! I think I left it on the kitchen table.
Kay: You're smiling, Jenny. I think you're happy about that.
Jenny: I'm sorry, Mom. But I have my book, so I can read.
Ted: Well, it'll be hard to read without a flashlight. What should we do now?

Lesson 30

A

Hi Harry! This is Max. Guess what! I have two job offers! I'm so happy, but I don't know which job to take. One is in Laketown, which is pretty far from here. It has so much beautiful scenery, but I think it's too quiet for me. There aren't many things to do there. There are no museums, no movie theaters and there are only a few restaurants. Also, the job doesn't pay much. I won't make much money in Laketown. But, a good thing about Laketown is that the air is so clean there. It doesn't have any air pollution at all.

The other job is in Central City. If I take the job in Central City, I'll make more money. I'll be near all my friends, and I can go out to eat at all the good restaurants. There are a lot of them in Central City. But as you know, Central City has a lot of crime and there aren't many cheap apartments. And the biggest problem in Central City is that there's too much traffic. I only have a few days to make my decision. What should I do? Give me a call when you can. Bye.

Lesson 31

A

I'm going to tell you a famous joke. Once upon a time, a mother mouse was running across the floor in the kitchen. The mother mouse was with her three children. Suddenly, the mother mouse heard a cat. The cat came into the kitchen. The baby mice were very scared. Then the mother mouse said, "Bow wow!" and the cat ran away. The mother mouse turned to her children and said, "See! I told you that it is very important to learn a foreign language!"

Lesson 33

A

Mark: It's a little cold here. Do you have another table?
Waiter: Well, right now there are only two other free tables. One is near the door, and the other one is over here, by the kitchen. Would you like that one?
Mark: Yes, we would. Thank you.
Waiter: We have two specials tonight. One is roast beef and the other is salmon.
Linda: I'll have the roast beef. And, sir, could you please get me another glass? This one is a little dirty.
Waiter: Oh, I'm sorry. Certainly!
Linda: Mark, I have some important news.
Mark: What is it?
Linda: We're going to have another baby!
Mark: Wow! That's great news!
Linda: I wonder if we'll have another son or another daughter . . . I'm so excited!

Review 29–33

A

Lily: I don't know what to study, Dad.
Dad: I can give you some ideas. How about biology? You can be a doctor.
Lily: No, doctors have too much work. I want to have a lot of free time to travel around the world.
Dad: I have another idea. How about English? You can be an English teacher.
Lily: Or a reporter. Reporters travel a lot.
Dad: Some reporters do. But most reporters don't make much money, you know.
Lily: I read that the reporters on Channel 4 make $100,000 a year.
Dad: Not all of them do. Only two reporters there make a lot of money. One makes $100,000 and the other makes $95,000. You should really do what makes you happy.

Lesson 34

A

Juan: I think we should buy an SUV. It's as big as a minivan, and we can drive it anywhere.

Maria: But an SUV isn't as safe as a minivan. SUVs roll over easily. We can get hurt. And a minivan holds more people.

Juan: Some SUVs carry as many passengers as a minivan. And you know I like to drive fast. A minivan doesn't go as fast as an SUV.

Maria: I don't care about speed. You know I don't drive as fast as you do. We have kids. I want a car that is as safe as the one we have now. And we need space for our luggage on trips. An SUV doesn't have as much space as a minivan. Also, SUVs are more expensive.

Juan: Well, an SUV has almost as much space as a minivan. But you're right, we should get the minivan. I want you to be happy.

Lesson 35

A

1. Ryan: The house on Elm Street is too small.
2. Katie: The house on 35th Avenue is too expensive.
3. Ryan: People drive too fast on Elm Street.
4. Katie: The neighborhood around Elm Street is safe enough.
5. Ryan: The house on Elm Street is too far from my work.
6. Katie: The house on Elm Street is close enough to the children's school.
7. Ryan: The house on 35th Avenue has a big enough yard for a dog.
8. Katie: The house on 35th Avenue isn't close enough to a bus stop.

Lesson 36

A

Miguel: I really miss Lima. I guess I feel a little homesick. I can't decide if I should stay here or go home.

Tim: Which city is more beautiful, Lima or San Francisco?

Miguel: To me, Lima is more beautiful. The buildings are older, but they're historical and interesting. The buildings in San Francisco are newer and more modern.

Tim: Which city has friendlier people?

Miguel: Well, I really think people in Lima are friendlier than the people in San Francisco, but maybe it's because I don't know many people yet.

Tim: That's probably the reason. It takes time to get to know people. I have another question for you. Which city is more convenient? You know, for shopping and getting around.

Miguel: That's hard to say. Public transportation in Lima is more convenient and stores stay open much later, so shopping is easier. But, the roads in Lima are narrower and there are no highways, so the traffic there is much worse than it is in San Francisco.

Tim: OK. One last question. What is something that you really, really miss about Lima?

Miguel: The food! Definitely the food! The food in Lima is spicier and more interesting. It's just much better overall.

Tim: You know, there are some Peruvian restaurants in San Francisco. Maybe you'll feel less homesick if you have some Peruvian food! Why don't we find a Peruvian restaurant to eat at tonight?

Lesson 37

A

East College has the lowest tuition, but it doesn't have a music program.

Central College has one of the best music programs, but it's the farthest from home.

West College has the least expensive dorms and food, but it has the highest tuition.

Central is the biggest college, and it has the most students. West College has the fewest students.

Review 34–37

A

I need to talk to Amy about our vacation. One of the most relaxing places is Coast Island, but it's also one of the most expensive places. Santa Costa is almost as expensive, but we saved enough money for a nice trip. I don't want to go anywhere that's too far or too hot. For me, beach vacations are better than going to the mountains. That's because I'm very lazy and all I want to do is just sit on a beach. My wife is much more energetic than I am, but she likes beaches too.

Lesson 39

A

Chen: Where's Ms. Kelly? It's time to start our test. She's never late, so I'm worried. Lily, what were you doing this morning? Did you see Ms. Kelly?

Lily: When I was walking across campus at 9:00, I saw her go into the library, so I know she's on campus. Ana, how about you? Were you studying in the library around 9:00?

Ana: No I wasn't. I was eating breakfast in the cafeteria with Jon. But I saw Ms. Kelly at 9:30. She was walking into the cafeteria at the same time we were walking out. Did you see her, Singh?

Singh: Yes, I did. I was buying books in the bookstore when she walked in.

Chen: What time were you buying books?

Singh: It was about 10:30. She was talking to some of our classmates. Hey, what about you, Chen? What were you doing this morning?

Chen: I was studying for the test, of course. I'm really worried about this test.

Lily: Where were you studying? What time was it? And did you see Ms. Kelly?

Chen: Well, it was about 11:00, and I was studying in an empty classroom. Ms. Kelly was walking down the hallway. She came into the classroom to get something.

Lily: How long did she stay?

Chen: I don't know, I left to come to class.

Lesson 40

A

Susan and Daniel's wedding was last Saturday night. At 7:30, everyone was sitting and waiting for the bride and groom. Finally, they came in. While Daniel was walking down the aisle, his parents were crying.

After the ceremony, everyone went into the reception hall. While they were dancing, Daniel's father stopped the band because he wanted to make a toast. When the room was quiet, everyone looked at the couple. Daniel's father held up his glass and wished the newlyweds a long, happy, and healthy life together. Everyone lifted up their glasses and said, "I'll drink to that!"

Lesson 38–40

A

It was a dark and stormy night. Eight hotel guests were sitting and talking by the fire. Some of them were drinking tea. Everyone looked worried. When lightening struck, everyone jumped. No one wanted to go upstairs to bed.

While the guests were talking, the hotel clerk came into the room and said, "Someone is at the door, and he is asking for Mr. Chambers." When he heard his name, Mr. Chambers didn't move. Everyone was looking at him, but he didn't get up. Then suddenly, . . .

Lesson 44

A

Ana: How about Saturday for the party? People won't be tired from work.

Sarah: Perfect. You know, we need some exciting activities for the kids so they won't be bored.

Ana: How about a piñata? They'll be excited to get candy and toys.

Sarah: Good idea! It'll be an interesting party because our neighbors come from so many different countries.

Ana: True. It'll be great to get to know everyone, and it'll help us feel safer.

Sarah: Yeah, after those frightening robberies in the neighborhood last month, I'm frightened at night when my husband is away.

Ana: I know what you mean. We'll all feel so much more relaxed when we get to know each other better. We can look out for each other.

Lesson 45

A

Dear Annie,

I am attending my last year of classes at my college. Finding a job that I really like worries me. Last year, I was working part-time at a software company while I was taking classes, but I wasn't happy. In fact, it was a very boring job. I realized that I like working with people more. Currently, I am taking a course called, "How to Teach Computer Literacy to Children." It's a very interesting class, and I love being with children. I'm wondering if I should stay in school longer. Teaching computers to children is what I really want to do. Is it too late to change direction?

Confused College Student

Review 41–45

A

At the end of a job interview, the interviewer usually asks if you have any questions. I recommend preparing a few questions ahead of time. Asking good questions can help you make a good impression. When you ask good questions, you show the employer that you are interested in the job. Not having questions prepared can be a problem. You'll have a hard time thinking of questions at the interview. I suggest asking what kind of employee does well at the company, and what the most interesting part of the job is. However, you need to avoid asking about salary and vacations. That information will come later. Following my advice will bring you success—I'm sure of that!

Lesson 46

A

Manuel: High school's finally over! I can't wait to start college in the fall. I want to finish quickly and go to medical school. I plan to find a cure for cancer and teach people to be healthy.

Yoshi: Are you crazy? School's over. We're finally free. I want to work in Europe, make money, and travel to Africa. I hope to see the world before I'm 25.

Manuel: How can you expect to be happy with no college education and no career?

Yoshi:I need to be free. That's what makes me happy.

Lesson 48

A

Yuko: Jin, when did you come to the U.S.?

Jin: About six months ago. And you?

Yuko: I came here three years ago. Why did you come, Jin?

Jin: I came here to be with my family. My sister came here 20 years ago, and then my mother came to help her take care of her kids. I finally decided to join my family. My other sisters are here and all of my aunts. What about you? Why did you come here?

Yuko: I came here to learn English and go to a university. I want to get a degree in business. My father has a company in Japan and I'm going to go back to work in his company. That's what *he* wants me to do anyway.

Jin: It sounds like a good plan. Is it what *you* really want to do? Usually *sons* work in their fathers' companies.

Yuko: I have a brother, but he's not interested. Anyway, my father thinks girls can do anything that boys can do. He sent me to good schools in Japan to get a good education. I'm glad he wants me to work with him. It's a good business and it's interesting.

Jin: Well, I'm happy for you. It's not easy to plan your future. I know I need to learn English to live here. So, here I am. Well, good luck this semester. It will be nice getting to know you.

Lesson 49

A

Alex: This line is so long. I don't like waiting in long lines. I especially can't stand being in line when it's so cold!

Tan: I know what you mean, but I really love seeing movies.

Alex: Not me, I'm here for my kids. I prefer reading.

Tan: Really? I love to go to the movies, especially action movies. But my wife told me that I can't continue to take the kids to those movies.

Alex: Why not?

Tan: Because they're so violent. She hates to let the kids see all that violence.

Alex: She's right. I like taking my kids to comedies. They won't have nightmares.

Tan: Oh look—the line started moving. Finally!

Review 46–49

A

Toby is using Get-A-Date.com to look for a girlfriend. Last year, he was happy to meet Nicole online, and they dated for a while. But they decided to break up after six months. Toby thinks it's important to stay friends with Nicole, so they have dinner together once in a while.

But now Toby is 30. He wants to get married, and his parents want him to get married. It's difficult to find the right person, but he is trying. He began looking a few weeks ago, and he will continue looking until he finds her.

Lesson 50

A

My name is Katrina, and I'm 44 years old. I have two jobs and take care of my family. I go to school at night to learn English. It's hard for

me to do all of the work for class. I try to turn in my homework on time, but sometimes I hand it in late. I try not to miss class because I know the teacher always passes out handouts, and I want to be there when she hands them out. I also need to be there to write down important information.

I'm always tired in class. Sometimes I don't understand the grammar lesson, and I have to figure it out at home. I look up new words in the dictionary, and sometimes I ask my son Frank to help me.

Lesson 51

A

Dear Fernanda,

Pablo's having a great time in Arizona. His first day of school was Monday. The boys got up early. They got on the bus near our house, and Pablo learned where to get off the bus when he goes to school by himself. At school, the teacher called on Pablo twice, and he answered in English

On Saturday, they ran into some of Carlos's friends, and the boys stayed out all day and played. The two boys came back around seven o'clock. Then we all ate out at our favorite pizzeria. When we came home, Carlos's cousin dropped by, and the three of them listened to music and played computer games. Pablo will fit in well. Everyone seems to like him. I know I do!

Maria

Lesson 53

A

Lucy: Well Mom, I'm all packed. I'm nervous about going, but I'm excited about my new job.

Mom: What are you nervous about? You're capable of doing anything you want. I'm so proud of you. You'll be fine, and this job is perfect for you. You're really good at what you do.

Lucy: Thanks, Mom. I'm sad about leaving my friends, but I'm happy about this new opportunity. I know I'll meet new people and I'm interested in learning about this new company. I'll be responsible for a lot.

Mom: You'll be great. Now let's go. There's a lot of traffic, and you don't want to be late for your flight.

Review 50–53

A

All day yesterday, I was looking forward to going to the theater after work. I was planning to eat out with my friend and then go to a really good show. When the elevator came, I was surprised by a noise it made, but I got on anyway. I was standing there and listening to someone's conversation when suddenly the elevator stopped. Everyone said, "Oh, no. Not again!" One guy said the elevator broke down last week. We were stuck in the elevator for three hours. I'm going to find out who's responsible for taking care of the building. I was very upset about missing dinner before the show.

Lesson 54

A

Jon: So, what did you want to show me, Rika?

Rika: That house. Look at it! It's strange. And my new neighbor is strange.

Jon: Why?

Rika: Well, I almost never see him.

Jon: So, he might be very busy. He could be at work a lot.

Rika: True. But I don't think he's home at night.

Jon: Well, he could be a doctor or a policeman. They often work at night.

Rika: I guess he could be. You know, he always keeps his curtains closed.

Jon: Well, he probably likes his privacy.

Rika: And he doesn't open his windows, even when it's hot outside.

Jon: So? He might not like noise. He may like peace and quiet.

Rika: And every time I look over there, I never see anyone.

Jon: He might live alone. A lot of people live alone. By the way, how old do you think he is?

Rika: Oh, he could be 40 or 50. He has some gray hair.

Jon: Well, I think you should just go introduce yourself to him. That way you can stop spending all your time wondering about him!

Lesson 55

A

Rika: I can't believe it, Jon. Another mystery in the neighborhood.

Jon: What is it now, Rika?

Rika: This dog showed up at our house, and we have no idea where he's from. He sure is cute.

Jon: He sure is. What do you know about him?

Rika: Well, he does everything we ask, so he must be well-trained. And he's not too thin, so he must eat well. He must come from a good home.

Jon: I see that he's great with your little sister and brother, so he must like kids.

Rika: He loves playing with them. And of course, they want to keep him.

Jon: What did you tell them?

Rika: I told them that he belongs to someone else who must be very upset right now.

Jon: I hope they understood. Does the dog have a name tag?

Rika: No. That's the problem. We don't know his name or anything about him. But he seems like a baby. He must not be very old.

Jon: What are you going to do?

Rika: I am thinking about taking his picture and putting up signs in the neighborhood. Do you have any suggestions?

Lesson 56

A

Francisco was born in the United States. Next month he's going to visit Argentina for the first time. Francisco's parents are from Argentina, and he wants to meet his relatives. He's a little nervous because he has a lot to do before he goes. He has to renew his passport for the trip because it expired, but he doesn't have to get a visa. He doesn't need a visa to go to Argentina.

His mother told him he should take gifts to his relatives because they like to get presents from the United States. It's winter in Argentina in July, so he shouldn't take summer clothes. He has to take warm clothes. He doesn't have to make hotel reservations because he can stay with relatives. His mom said he shouldn't take a lot of cash. Instead, he should take his ATM card. He knows he should go to bed early the night before the flight because it's a long trip.

Lesson 57

A

Carol: What do we have to do before we can move in? And what should we do after we move in?

Mike: Well, we have to buy a new stove now because the house doesn't have one.

Carol: Should we buy a new refrigerator? I know our refrigerator is OK, but it's not new.

Mike: Well, it still works, so we don't have to buy one now. I think we should buy a new refrigerator later. Tell me, do you think we should paint the outside of the house?

Carol: Yes, definitely. We don't have to do it now, but we should do it before winter. The old paint doesn't look very good, and it will rain a lot. Do you think we should paint the inside rooms now?

Mike: Hmm. I think we should wait. There are other things we have to do first. Two of the windows are broken. I think we have to buy new windows before we move in.

Carol: You're right. And we have to buy a new bed for the guest room because Billy and Betty are coming to stay with us next week. And we have to buy a new dishwasher. I hate to do dishes. When should we buy one?

Mike: Do we have to buy one, or do you just *want* to buy one? Don't forget that the roof leaks and we have to fix it right away. I think we should wait before we buy the dishwasher. I'll be your dishwasher.

Carol: Honey, it's a deal.

Lesson 58

A

Tran: Hi, Susana. How are you? I'm so happy to see you!

Susana: Tran! You look great! What are you doing these days?

Tran: Well, you know, I used to be a gymnastics teacher. But last year I decided to open my own gym.

Susana: Wow! That's terrific! I should go to your gym. I need some exercise.

Tran: I hope you do! So, what's new with you? Did you graduate?

Susana: Yes, last month. Now I'm looking for a job in a hospital.

Tran: I'm sure you'll get a job soon.

Review 54–58

A

Bill: Hey Bob! You shouldn't throw those newspapers away.

Bob: I know. I should recycle them, but I don't know how.

Bill: Ask your landlord. There must be some recycling containers around here.

Bob: I looked, but I didn't see any.

Bill: They might be behind that wall. I'll check . . .Yup! There they are. I knew it! See—you have to look around and ask questions when you move in.

Bob: I know. But you know how shy I am. Thanks for helping me out.

Lesson 60

A

Denise: How long have you been in Boston?

Alberto: I've been here since January. But I haven't had a job since I left my country.

Denise: Where are you from?

Alberto: I'm from Brazil. I grew up in Sao Paolo.

Denise: Really? I'm from Argentina. I've been to Brazil many times, but I haven't been to Sao Paulo. I haven't been back to Argentina for ten years.

Alberto: Wow! That's a long time.

Denise: I know! I'm thinking about going next summer. Now, tell me, have you had any experience working in a salon before? This job requires three years of experience.

Alberto: Yes. I've worked in this profession for twelve years. I have a lot of experience.

Denise: What skills do you have?

Alberto: Well, I've cut and styled hair for a long time. I can also color hair.

Denise: That's great. By the way, your English is very good.

Alberto: Thanks. I've been an ESL student for five months. I also studied English in Brazil.

Denise: Great! I also need someone who can make phone calls to remind clients about their appointments. And some clients ask for make-up. Can you do that, too?

Alberto: Oh yes. I've done make-up for many years. And to answer your question about the phone, well, I haven't spoken in English very much on the phone since I came to this country, but I can understand a lot. It won't be a problem.

Denise: Well, everything sounds great. You're hired. Can you start on Monday?

Alberto: Thank you! Yes! What time should I come in?

Lesson 61

A

Ali: Hey Ted, let's make plans for the weekend. What do you want to do? We can go to Wild World Amusement Park. Have you ever been on a roller coaster?

Ted: Yes, I have. Once. And I'll never do it again. I got sick.

Ali: OK. How about the beach? Have you ever gone surfing? It's fantastic. I love surfing.

Ted: No, I haven't. I'm too scared. There are sharks in the ocean. I've hardly ever gone swimming in the ocean. Pools are safer.

Ali: Have you ever climbed a mountain? It's wonderful when you get to the top. You can see for miles.

Ted: Are you crazy? I've never done that. It's so dangerous!

Ali: No it's not. I usually go climbing with a group. We help each other out. Well, how about this—have you ever jumped out of a plane with a parachute, or taken a hot air balloon ride? I've done both. The views are fantastic.

Ted: No, I haven't. I'd like to live past the age of 30.
Ali: Well, I'm out of ideas. How about a movie?
Ted: Perfect!

Review 59–61

A

Have you ever fallen in love at first sight? Well, I never have. I know it happens in the movies. My cousin always falls in love immediately, but she has been married and divorced three times! You know what? She's in love again, and she has known the guy for only two weeks. She has been this way since she was a teenager. My brother has tried to give her advice, but she doesn't listen. Oh well. I hope she has found the right guy this time.

Lesson 62

A

Chang: So, Victor, how's it going? Have you registered for your classes yet?
Victor: Yes, I have. I can't believe I'm taking five classes!
Chang: Oh, you won't have any trouble. You'll do fine. Have you bought your books yet?
Victor: No, I haven't. I went to the bookstore yesterday, but the line was too long.
Chang: I know. It's terrible. Maybe we should try later. Hey—I'm going over to the club office later to join the International Students Club. Do you want to come with me?
Victor: Thanks, but I've already joined the club.
Chang: Wow! You don't waste any time, Victor!
Victor: Well, I like to take care of things as soon as I can.
Chang: I should try to be like you. Anyway, listen. I saw Eva yester-

day and she asked about you. Why haven't you called her yet? You know she's back from her trip.
Victor: Eva? Well, I know she's back. I haven't called her yet . . . because I met someone else this summer . . .
Chang: You're dating someone else already? So why haven't you told her about this yet? She should know!
Victor: You're right. I'll give her a call tonight.

Lesson 63

A

Pedro: Have you watched any of the World Cup? It's been on TV for the past two weeks.
Kim: Uh-huh! I haven't missed a game. I love soccer. I play on my school team.
Pedro: Really? How long have you played on the team?
Kim: For about five years. I'm the goalie.
Pedro: Wow! How long have you been the goalie?
Kim: Since my first year on the team.
Pedro: How many times has your team won this year?
Kim: You won't believe this, but we've won ten games.
Pedro: That's great. Do you travel to other cities for games?
Kim: Yeah, all the time.
Pedro: Wow! How many times have you done that?
Kim: A lot. We've traveled all over the country. We've traveled to about 20 games this year. I think we've been to 20 states.
Pedro: You've seen a lot of the country! I'm jealous! I love to watch soccer. I go to lots of games. In fact, I've already been to six games this year.
Kim: Have you ever tried to play?
Pedro: Yes, I've played for two years. I'm terrible. But I'm good at watching! When's your next

game? I'd love to see you play.
Kim: We have a home game next Saturday at 2:00. Can you come?
Pedro: I think so. I'll let you know.

Review 62–64

A

Interviewer: Thank you for letting me interview you.
Mr. Wilson: No problem. We're always happy to give interviews.
Interviewer: How many times have you given interviews before?
Mrs. Wilson: Oh, five or six in the last ten years, I think. We're happy to talk about our lives.
Interviewer: That's great. So tell me, you're both 101 years old, right?
Mr. Wilson: That's right.
Interviewer: And how long have you been married?
Mrs. Wilson: Ahhh…We've been happily married for 79 years.
Interviewer: Have you started planning a party yet for your 80th anniversary?
Mrs. Wilson: No, *we* haven't, but two of our great grandchildren have. They have already reserved a restaurant.
Mr. Wilson: But they haven't sent out the invitations yet.
Mrs. Wilson: Don't worry, dear. They will.
Interviewer: And here's another question . . .

Index